OPERATIVE CREAMERY

CREAMERY

PRODUCE OF
THE REPUBLIC OF IRELAND

DAIRY SOCIETY

MERY BUTTER

grove
Y CO.
CO. KERRY.

REAMERY.
Kerry

ry Butter

ord

MILD

Reg. No. C288

TOHER
BRAND

MILD

FINEST IRISH CREAMERY BUTTER

Ballyragget Co-op. Creamery Ltd.

CO KILKENNY

Reg. No. C150.

Castlelyons

PURE IRISH CREAMERY BUTTER
CASTLELYONS CO-OP CREAMERY LTD
CASTLELYONS, CO. CORK

KANTOHER CREAMERIES
ADDED INGREDIENT SALT Reg. No. C297
KILLEDY, BALLAGH, LIMERICK.

GOLDEN VEIN

BALLYHANILL

CHOICES

BANDON CO-OP
AGRICUL
SPE

Pure Irish

1 lb. Nett

SHA

CMD
TRADE MARK

THE GREAT IRISH BUCKET LIST

Gill Books
Hume Avenue, Park West, Dublin 12

www.gillbooks.ie

Gill Books is an imprint of M.H. Gill & Co.

Copyright © Teapot Press Ltd 2024

ISBN: 978-1-8045-8089-9

This book was created and produced by Teapot Press Ltd

Text by Catherine Gough
Designed by Tony Potter

Printed in the EU

This book is typeset in Noto Serif, Futura PT and Fields Display

5 4 3 2 1

THE GREAT IRISH BUCKET LIST

Catherine Gough

Gill Books

101 unmissable adventures

Ulster

Connacht

Leinster

Munster

DONEGAL

DERRY

ANTRIM

TYRONE

DOWN

FERMANAGH

ARMAGH

SLIGO

MONAGHAN

LEITRIM

CAVAN

MAYO

LOUTH

ROSCOMMON

LONGFORD

MEATH

WESTMEATH

GALWAY

OFFALY

DUBLIN

KILDARE

WICKLOW

LAOIS

CLARE

CARLOW

LIMERICK

TIPPERARY

KILKENNY

WEXFORD

KERRY

WATERFORD

CORK

Introduction

A small island with a big history, Ireland has an array of attractions that range from spectacular geological formations and mysterious ancient structures to innovative art installations and mind-opening museums. There's so much to see and do, and with an island so compact it is all within easy reach.

Sunset at Murder Hole Beach, Boyeeghter Bay, Co. Donegal.

In *The Great Irish Bucket List*, you'll find a list of 101 attractions that can't be missed. There are lots of old familiars, which are popular for a very good reason, such as the Cliffs of Moher, formed 320 million years ago on the Atlantic coast, and Newgrange, a passage tomb that's older than the pyramids and holds just as many secrets. There are also plenty of hidden gems, such as St Michan's Mummies in Dublin, a church crypt where decaying coffins have revealed mummified bodies, as well as experiences that will take you off the beaten track, such as The Gobbins cliff path in Antrim, an exhilarating walk along a structure hanging from a cliff face.

Ireland's natural wonders and national parks provide for breathtaking scenery and outdoor exploits, and there are hiking trails, waterfalls, and beaches galore to be explored. The unique habitat of the Burren in Clare is home to plant life that can be found nowhere else in Ireland, and Murder Hole Beach is a must for a brisk walk on the sublime Donegal coast, the beach's name as intriguing as it is terrifying.

Many of Ireland's beautiful locations are steeped in folklore, with the vast and colourful Irish legends rivalling that of Greek and Norse mythology. You can't visit the Giant's Causeway in Antrim without hearing about the legend of how its basalt columns were created as a pathway to Scotland so Irish warrior Fionn mac Cumhaill could battle the Scottish giant Benandonner. And the lesser-known Cave of the Cats in Roscommon, associated with the fabled Queen Medb, was thought to be a portal to the mythological Otherworld.

There are archaeological sites at every turn in Ireland, with cairns and dolmens peppering the landscape, some giving small clues to the mystery of how, and why, they came to be. The nation's long history, too, is written into its towns and cities, with museums, such as the award-winning *Titanic* Belfast and the unconventional Butter Museum in Cork, providing windows to Ireland's past.

The book has been divided into the four provinces of Ireland, with sections covering Natural Wonders, Unique Ireland, the Great Outdoors, and Culture and Craic, so there are a variety of options, no matter where you find yourself. Of course, many things have been left out, which is simply down to space. For example, the Blarney Stone in Cork, which is already well known, and Puck Fair in Kerry, one of Ireland's oldest festivals. However, with 101 things up your sleeve, there is more than enough to make your visit unforgettable, whether you're a road-tripping local or an overseas guest.

You can drive from Malin Head in the north to Mizen Head in the south in about eight hours, so no matter where your base you can head off at a moment's notice in search of new places and new experiences. To start off, here are three nationwide events that take place annually, so you can plan your visit to coincide with these quintessential Irish festivals.

Adventure awaits . . .

Opposite: Sea cliffs at Malin Head, the northernmost point in Ireland.

01 Culture Night

Enjoy Ireland's arts and heritage – September

Culture Night is undoubtedly the best night in Ireland's cultural calendar. For one evening in September every year, venues across the country open late and for free, giving the public access to the nation's top tourist attractions as well as local gems.

It started in 2006 as an initiative of Temple Bar Cultural Trust and Dublin City Council, and from its modest beginnings in Dublin it spread to counties and towns across Ireland, encompassing Gaeltacht regions and remote islands. It launched an international event in 2012 and Liverpool, Leeds, London, and Newcastle held Irish Culture Nights, with the event spreading as far as New York in 2017.

There were 1,700 Culture Night events in 2023, with over 1.2 million people in attendance. The events are broad, showcasing dance, literature, history, and art, among many other things, honouring the rich and varied culture in Ireland today. The night aims to celebrate community and it centres on inclusivity, opening pathways of discovery and engagement for all who call Ireland their home.

For a country already known for its rich heritage, Culture Night condenses it all into a single festival that floods Ireland's towns with creativity. You can choose what to do from the extensive programme of events, or simply wander about your town or city taking it all in. Public spaces are taken over by performers and audiences, and Ireland's extraordinary museums and galleries leave their doors open, shining light into the dark September night.

Opposite: Traditional Irish music is one of the features of Culture Night.

02 St Patrick's Day

The parade of parades — 17 March

St Patrick's Day, originally a religious holiday, has become so deeply embedded in Irish culture that it is almost more Irish than Ireland itself. It is celebrated in more countries than any other national festival, and how we mark the occasion today was heavily influenced by the Irish diaspora, with Boston holding its first St Patrick's Day parade as far back as 1737. Ireland didn't hold its first parade until 1903, when Waterford held a procession to mark Irish Language Week.

Now it is estimated that 500,000 people attend the main St Patrick's Day parade on 17 March in Dublin city centre. Tourists arrive like an avalanche on the city to join in the festivities, and the televised parade is a worthy spectacle. Every year it showcases the best of Ireland's creative talent through the unique displays, and gaggles of visiting American brass bands march their way through the Dublin streets, rain, hail, or shine.

However, the heart of St Patrick's Day is in the small-town celebrations around the country, with floats from local businesses, bunting-clad tractors, and children's dance groups filling the streets. Two noteworthy parades are the one in Dripsey, Co. Cork, which once held the record for the shortest parade in Ireland, travelling less than 25 metres, and the one in Dingle, Co. Kerry, which starts at 6 a.m. with a strike of the big drum by the Dingle Fife and Drum Band.

The floats that roll through the streets of the regional parades are some of the most iconic and culturally timely creations. Politicians are poked fun at, viral cultural moments are recreated, and famous works of art are paid homage to. So while the spectacle of the 'official' parade in Dublin is worth the trip, keeping it local can offer a one-of-a-kind experience.

Marching dancers at the St Patrick's Day Parade in Dublin.

03 Fleadh Cheoil

Music and more — August

The Fleadh Cheoil was first held in 1951 in Mullingar, Co. Westmeath, where only a few hundred people attended. Every year since, a new town on the island of Ireland has hosted the summer event. It is the biggest celebration of Irish traditional music, dance, and language in the world, with every street corner, concert hall, school, pub, and snug in the host town fizzing with sound for the week-long festival.

The largest events to date have attracted upwards of 500,000 attendees, with the pinnacle of traditional Irish music talent on show. The origins of the festival, however, are as a competition, developed to establish standards in Irish traditional music. And the competition lives on, with competitors battling through rounds of regional contests before they can test their skills at the Fleadh Cheoil. Musicians from all over Ireland, and all over the world, descend on the host town with their fiddles, bodhráns, whistles, and harps, and when the competitions are over for the day, there are impromptu *seisiúns* where trad musicians young and old play for pleasure.

The Fleadh Cheoil has an abiding legacy, and it only seems to be growing in popularity. The festival is as great for spectators as it is for musicians, with concerts, parades, 'try an instrument' sessions, and céilís throughout the week. But at the heart of the Fleadh Cheoil is connection – it is a time for the musicians to connect with each other, for the spectators to connect with the melodies, and for Ireland to connect with its traditional music legacy.

Young musicians performing on the streets of Drogheda at the Fleadh
Cheoil na Éireann Drogheda 2018 Irish cultural music and dance festival.

Natural Wonders

Great Sugarloaf mountain in Co. Wicklow.

Unique Ireland

Interior of the Old Library, Trinity College, Dublin.

The Great Outdoors

Curracloe Beach in Co. Wexford.

Culture and Craic

Two monks carved in stone, one holding a cross, the other holding a roll, Jerpoint Abbey, Co. Kilkenny.

04 Dunmore Cave

Co. Kilkenny

Dunmore Cave may not be one of Ireland's biggest caves, but it houses some of the finest calcite formations you can see. The most notable of these is the Market Cross, standing at 5.8 metres and named for its distinctive cross shape. The passages and chambers of the cave were formed over millions of years by glacial meltwaters, and the cave's long history is notable not just in its geological formations, but in its archaeological significance, too.

The cave is mentioned in a collection of writing known as *The Triads of Ireland,* thought to date back to the 9th century, where it is named as 'one of the three darkest places in Ireland'. It is also mentioned in the 17th century *Annals of the Four Masters,* chronicles of Irish medieval history, as the site of a Viking massacre in 928 AD. The Annals state that 1,000 people were killed in the Viking massacre, and human remains found in the cave were thought to be related to this, though archaeologists haven't been able to confirm it.

In recent history, a hoard of silver and bronze items was found deep in the cave during an excavation in 1999, which archaeologists have dated to around 970 AD.

With Dunmore Cave's dark history in its past, it is now a show cave equipped with stairs and lighting to view the amazing calcite columns, and it has a visitor's centre so you can learn about the history of this natural wonder.

Interior of Dunmore Cave.

05 Saltee Islands

Co. Wexford

Off the coast of Co. Wexford, nestled in St George's Channel, the Saltee Islands are a short 20-minute ferry trip from the mainland. The islands lie on an important migratory route, so they are a haven for many bird species, as well as a breeding ground for grey seals.

The islands consist of Great Saltee and Little Saltee, though it's not possible to visit Little Saltee due to hazardous landing conditions. Great Saltee, however, provides more than enough breathtaking scenery, as well as being a popular bird sanctuary. During the spring and autumn bird migrations, you can see gannets, Manx shearwaters, razorbills, and puffins. The puffins alone can provide hours of bird-watching, as they're used to the presence of day-trippers. Special Protection Area status was awarded to the islands and its surrounding waters to conserve the habitat.

Great Saltee Island.

Leinster • Natural Wonders

Puffiins feeding on fish in the Saltee Islands.

The islands are thought to be between 600 million and 2 billion years old, and traces of a fort, remains of an ancient grave, and an ogham stone suggest human settlement. Due to their position along a once important sea-trading route between Britain and America, the island is also thought to have been a base for pirates and smugglers.

The seas around the islands are as blue and clear as any you will find in sunnier climates, though they can be treacherous, leading to the legend that the area was once known as 'graveyard of a thousand ships and the islands their tombstones'.

06 Rock of Dunamase

Co. Laois

The Rock of Dunamase is a prominent, rocky outcrop in Co. Laois, from which you can take in spectacular views of the surrounding countryside and beyond to the Slieve Bloom Mountains. But our Irish ancestors weren't interested in the Rock for its sights. As an early Christian settlement, it was known as Dun Masc or Masc's Fort, which was pillaged by Vikings in 842.

When the Normans arrived in Ireland in the 12th century, it became an important Anglo-Norman stronghold. A castle was built on the Rock of Dunamase in the latter half of the 12th century, the defensive features of which made use of the unique topography.

Dermot MacMurrough, King of Leinster, included Dunamase

Leinster • Natural Wonders

as part of his daughter Aoife's dowry when she was promised in marriage to the Norman conqueror Strongbow. Aoife and Strongbow went on to have a daughter called Isabel, and Dunamase was given as part of her wedding gift for her marriage to William Marshal, 1st Earl of Pembroke.

The castle passed through the ownership of a number of wealthy families, including the O'Moores, until it was eventually blown up in 1650 during the Cromwellian conquest of Ireland. The castle has fallen into disrepair, the Rock strewn with the debris of history, but the ruins still exude an arresting atmosphere. You can walk through the barbican gate, which apparently contained a murder hole through which stones and boiling water could be thrown on intruders below. Now it stands crumbling on the pathway to the once-imposing fort.

The ruins of the castle on the Rock of Dunamase.

07 Powerscourt Waterfall

Co. Wicklow

Powerscourt Waterfall is a dramatic cascade of water on the Powerscourt Estate near the foothills of the Wicklow Mountains. One of Ireland's largest waterfalls, it is known as a 'horsetail', as the water stays in contact with the rock as it descends. Here the River Dargle plummets from a height of 121 metres, surrounded by an open area that's perfect for picnics and lush woodlands that boast pines, oaks, and even giant redwoods.

08 The Great Sugarloaf

Co. Wicklow

Standing at only 501 metres high, it is its conical shape that makes the Great Sugarloaf so identifiable. It sits apart from the Wicklow Mountains, and is a relatively easy climb, with a bit of a scramble on the last leg due to rocky terrain. When you reach the top, you will be rewarded with views of Dublin City and the Wicklow Mountains, and, if it's a clear day, you can even spot the Mourne Mountains in Co. Down and Snowdonia in Wales.

09 Lough Tay

Co. Wicklow

Lough Tay is located in the Wicklow Mountains, close to Glendalough. It is one of the most photographed places in Wicklow, with the still lake surrounded by the Djouce and Luggala mountains offering a stunning panoramic view. The lake is nicknamed the 'Guinness Lake' due to its dark colour and white sandy beach giving it the look of a pint of Guinness. It was also part of the Guinness Estate at Luggala from 1937 until its sale in 2019.

Powerscourt Waterfall, with its 121-metre drop.

Leinster • Natural Wonders

10 Newgrange

Co. Meath

It's unlikely there is a single person in Ireland without winter solstice at Newgrange on their bucket list. A 5,200-year-old passage tomb in the Boyne Valley, Newgrange is older than both Stonehenge and the Giza pyramids. A 19-metre-long passage leads to a chamber with a high corbelled roof and three alcoves, where bones and possible votive offerings were discovered. Outside, beyond the large, circular mound, it is surrounded by kerbstones engraved with Neolithic art. The most spectacular of these is the five-tonne entrance stone, displaying a triple-spiral design.

But the description hardly does it justice. Newgrange is a deeply striking place where ritual meets science. On the shortest day of the year, the first light of the rising sun pierces the roof box and expands through the passage, illuminating the chamber beyond. Astronomical alignment and spiritual belief go hand in hand at the site on the winter solstice, and to be there to experience it is to take a step back in time.

One of three sites in Brú na Bóinne, an ancient monument complex that attracts 200,000 visitors a year, Newgrange was designated a UNESCO World Heritage Site. Tickets for the winter solstice event are distributed by lottery, with around 30,000 applicants but only 50 tickets available. In Irish mythology, Newgrange is sometimes spoken of as a portal to the Otherworld, and to be one of the lucky few to be there on winter solstice is to see why.

Opposite: lucky lottery winners witness the first rays of sun inside the tomb.

Below: The stars above Newgrange.

11 The Long Room, Trinity College
Co. Dublin

Part of the Old Library in Trinity College Dublin, the Long Room is one of the most beautiful libraries in the world. The barrel-shaped ceiling of the almost 65-metre-long room is spectacular, and the marble busts of writers and philosophers lining the walkway are like sentries protecting the shelves upon shelves of old books. The collection consists of 200,000 books, among which is one of the few remaining copies of the 1916 Proclamation of the Irish Republic. It also houses the 'Brian Boru' harp, one of the oldest of its kind in Ireland and thought to date to the 15th century.

When the library was built in the 1700s, it had a flat ceiling, and the books were shelved on the lower level only. As the collection grew, the distinctive barrel ceiling for which the library has become instantly recognisable was created, and the collection was expanded to the upper levels. The library also hosts temporary exhibitions, often displaying unique and rare manuscripts.

Just outside the entrance to the Long Room, the Book of Kells is on permanent display. It is a lavishly decorated 9th-century manuscript with both Celtic and Christian iconography. It is composed of the four gospels, hand-written onto vellum, and named for the monastery in Kells, Co. Meath, where the manuscript was held for centuries after a Viking raid.

The barrel-shaped ceiling of the Long Room, with thousands of books lining the shelves below.

12 All-Ireland Final in Croke Park

Co. Dublin

Many GAA fans would sell their grandmother for a ticket to an All-Ireland final in Croke Park; the tickets are gold dust, and the experience is priceless. Gaelic games are rooted not just in Irish sporting history, but also in Irish mythology, with demigod Cú Chulainn said to be handy with a sliotar and hurley.

Croke Park, the headquarters of the Gaelic Athletics Association (GAA), is the fourth-largest stadium in Europe, and when the All-Ireland Championships come around, fans arrive in their droves, decked out in the colours of their counties, to witness the clash of a lifetime.

The GAA was founded in 1884 to nurture traditional sports and make them accessible to all, no matter their social standing, and it is now one of the most celebrated amateur sporting associations in the world. There are over 2,200 clubs in Ireland, with hundreds around the globe. Whether Gaelic football, hurling, camogie or ladies' Gaelic football, the All-Ireland finals draw county pride out in all, with even occasional fans coming out of the woodwork trying to get a ticket.

With a capacity of 82,300, attendance numbers at the All-Ireland finals in Croke Park can be mammoth. The games are deeply embedded in the Irish psyche, and the intensity with which the teams play is second only to the passion of the fans.

Leinster • Unique Ireland

A marching band lead Galway and Kerry teams around the pitch at an All-Ireland final in Croke Park, Dublin.

13 Trim Castle

Co. Meath

An imposing presence on the south bank of the River Boyne, Trim Castle is one of the largest and most well-preserved Anglo-Norman castles in Ireland. Built in 1172 by Hugh de Lacy, Lord of Meath, the original wooden structure was burnt down a few years later by the High King of Ireland, Ruaidrí Ua Conchobair. Rebuilt in stone, three of the four towers still stand, and you can wander the impressive 20-sided keep, which kept the de Lacys safe within. The Office of Public Works began a major programme of conservation in the 1990s, and the castle was re-opened to the public in 2000.

Trim Castle.

14 St Michan's Mummies

Co. Dublin

Originally founded in 1095, St Michan's long history has revealed itself in a truly unique way. The wood of the coffins strewn about the church's crypt has disintegrated, revealing mummified bodies. In some caskets you can see part of an arm or leg, but others are chillingly visible. The most famous of these, known as the 'big four', are called the Unknown, the Thief, the Nun, and the Crusader, the latter being a staggering six and a half feet tall, with his legs folded under him to fit in the small coffin.

In 2019, the head of the Crusader was stolen during a break-in and his body badly damaged, but the head has since been retrieved.

15 St Audoen's Gate

Co. Dublin

A formidable stone wall once enveloped the medieval city of Dublin, which was accessible only through a set of archways. The wall was built in the mid-1200s by the Normans, and as the need for Dublin to protect itself diminished, so too did the wall. Only small sections of it remain, including St Audoen's Gate. Nestled behind a church, the arch leads to a small pathway by which city-dwellers can reach the areas of High Street and Cornmarket.

St Audoen's Church from a stone arch entrance.

Leinster • Unique Ireland

Some of the Dead Zoo residents at Ireland's
Natural History Museum on Merrion Street, Dublin.

16 The Dead Zoo

Co. Dublin

The Natural History Museum in Dublin, known locally as 'the
Dead Zoo', is a cabinet-style museum which showcases a collection
of minerals and other items such as taxidermy and skeletons of
animals, including a composite of the extinct dodo. One of the
most intriguing features of the Dead Zoo is that it is a museum of a
museum – the display today is as it was at the turn of the century,
with whale and shark skeletons suspended from the ceiling, and
some of the animals showing evidence of the bullets that killed them.

17 Glendalough

Co. Wicklow

Nature and heritage come together in the 'valley of the two lakes'. In this breathtaking valley carved by glaciers stands a monastic city. A cathedral, a smattering of chapels, a stone cross and a 30-metre-high round tower all take pride of place among the lush woods of Glendalough. St Kevin founded the monastery here in the 6th century, and it is easy to see why he chose the location.

As well as taking in the delicate stonework of the monastic structures, most of which date back to the 10th to 12th centuries, Glendalough is the perfect place to retreat from the city and explore the outdoors. There are numerous walking routes, each varying in difficulty, each worth the effort. You can hike to the beautiful Poulanass Waterfall and plunge pools, and on to the Upper Lake and Lugduff Mountain, or explore the lush woodlands to see if you can spot red deer. There's even a deserted Miners Village.

The Upper and Lower Lakes are worth viewing any time of the year, and you can roll up your trousers and dip your toes in the cool water after the walk. Descending through the oak forest, it's the perfect place to be still and feel the tranquillity that the monks must have felt all those centuries ago.

Glendalough from the air.

18 The Wicklow Way

Co. Dublin to Co. Carlow

The Wicklow Way is around 130 kilometres long and can take between five and ten days to complete. Established in 1980, it was the first sign-posted long-distance walking trail in Ireland, and it is now one of the most popular routes on the island. It starts from the suburbs of Dublin, traversing the Wicklow Mountains, and down into Co. Carlow, where it ends in the village of Clonegal.

The trail takes you through quiet woodlands, mountain paths, and along country roads, and on the route you can take in views of crystal-clear lakes, glacial valleys, rich vegetation, and roaring waterfalls. The Wicklow Mountains National Park is a protected area, and beautiful varieties of heathers and gorse dominate the mountainsides, while peregrine falcons nest on the cliffs.

Walking the Wicklow Way isn't for the faint-hearted, and some sections of it will challenge your physical endurance. However, the route is easily accessible, so it's possible to walk the trail in sections over a longer period of time.

Some of the most notable sites along the trail are Powerscourt Estate, Glendalough, Lough Tay, Djouce Mountain, and the Bronze Age cairn at Two Rock. You can take a break on one of the picnic benches along the way to refresh in the outdoors, or even have a well-deserved pint in Johnnie Fox's pub.

Leinster • The Great Outdoors

Wooden path on the
Wicklow Way.

40

19 Mount Usher Gardens

Co. Wicklow

Set on the banks of the River Vartry in Ashford, Mount Usher Gardens is one of the finest examples of a 'Robinsonian' garden in existence today. William Robinson, an Irish gardener and journalist, came up with the concept of a 'managed wild' garden, that complements its natural setting. The Walpole family were inspired by this and began designing a garden in the late 19th century. Today the gardens house almost 5,000 different species over 22 acres of land. *Gardeners' World* presenter Monty Don has named Mount Usher as one of his favourite gardens.

The meandering paths lead you through a spectrum of colour, with groves, glades, and bridges over tumbling water. The gardens have extensive collections of rhododendrons, azaleas, magnolias and camellias, and on the tree walks you can marvel at the size of the evergreen Nothofagus fusca, also known as red beech, and take in the scent of Eucalyptus.

The gardens are also home to Ireland's biggest trees, known as 'champion trees', and as well as home-grown species, wildflowers are encouraged and wildlife thrives.

It is a vibrant garden, perfect for wandering in any season. In spring, the purple and white crocuses come to life along the Palm Walk. In summer, the palette changes and rhododendrons and azaleas reveal their colours. Then in autumn, the garden mellows and it's a perfect time for the Maple Walk, while keeping an eye out for mushrooms cropping up at ground level.

Nyssa sylvatica, also known as tupelo or blackgum, with beautiful autumnal red leaves at Mount Usher Gardens.

Leinster • The Great Outdoors

20 River Barrow

Co. Carlow

The River Barrow is the longest of the Three Sisters, and the second-longest river in Ireland. With its source high in the Slieve Bloom Mountains, the river is navigable from Athy in Kildare to St Mullins in Carlow, and the best way to experience it is by boat. The waterway will take you on a serene journey past ancient sites, beautiful woodlands, and historic towns. It's even possible to explore the Barrow by canoe, spotting kingfishers and otters on the open water.

21 Ireland's Eye

Co. Dublin

Just off the coast of Howth and accessible by a short boat journey, Ireland's Eye is a long-uninhabited island teeming with wildlife. The summit can be reached in 20 minutes, from where you can view the spectacular freestanding rock known as 'the Stack'. A Martello tower and ruins of a church are the only evidence of human activity on the island, which has now been taken over by a colony of grey seals and thousands of guillemots, gannets, razorbills, fulmars and gulls.

A Martello tower on Ireland's Eye.

22 Curracloe Beach

Co. Wexford

Curracloe is a gorgeous stretch of beach with fine, white sand not far from Wexford Town. The beach takes up a noteworthy 11 kilometres of the coastline, and from it you can reach Raven Nature Reserve, which is part of a protected sand-dune system. Curracloe is also famous for appearing in the opening scenes of *Saving Private Ryan,* but it's the bracing walk along golden sand that will capture your imagination.

Two people stroll along the beautiful sands on Curracloe Beach.

23 Kilmainham Gaol

Co. Dublin

Kilmainham Gaol, opened in 1796, once held thousands of men, women and children behind its thick walls. Most were petty criminals, some even committing crimes on purpose during the Famine years in the hopes of being fed while imprisoned. It was also used as a holding place for criminals who were sentenced for transportation to Australia, as well as beggars and those with mental illnesses, which led to severe overcrowding. Cells designed for one person often held up to five prisoners. Conditions in the prison were woeful, particularly for women and children who were kept in the dark and old West Wing.

Some prisoners were sentenced to hard labour while in the gaol, which meant laundry duty for women and stone-breaking for men. The latter was carried out in one of the gaol's yards, which became known as the Stonebreakers' Yard. This yard is where 14 of the leaders of the 1916 Rising were executed by firing squad.

The rebellion leaders of the Rising were arrested, tried in secret, and sentenced to death before being transferred to Kilmainham, where they got to say their goodbyes to loved ones. One of the prisoners, Joseph Plunkett, married his partner, Grace Gifford, in the gaol chapel the night before his execution.

The gaol later housed Republican prisoners, detained by the Free State Army. The Republican leader Éamon de Valera was one of the last prisoners to leave the gaol in 1924 before it fell into abandonment. Now the gaol is a museum where visitors can learn about its infamous history. Kilmainham Gaol first opened to the public in 1966.

Kilmainham Gaol main hall.

Leinster • Culture and Craic

24 Jerpoint Abbey

Co. Kilkenny

Dating back to the latter part of the 12th century, Jerpoint Abbey is one of the best-preserved ruins in Ireland. The architecture and carvings are remarkably intact, and walking among them gives visitors a glimpse into what life was like for the Cistercian monks who founded the abbey centuries ago.

The abbey was constructed by the King of the Kingdom of Ossory, Donogh O'Donoghoe Mac Gilla Pátraic, and he moved a sect of Cistercian monks to the Kilkenny site in 1180. It was active until King Henry VIII's dissolution of monasteries, when it was surrendered by the abbot, Oliver Grace. Jerpoint was given to James Butler, the 9th Earl of Ormond, in 1541, and was primarily used as a place of internment.

The Romanesque church as you see it today dates from the 12th century, and the tower is from the 15th century. However, the abbey is mostly known for its beautiful stone carvings and sculptures. Jerpoint houses the adorned tomb of the abbey's first abbot, Felix O'Dulany, and the pillars of the cloister arcade are decorated with detailed carvings. Walking among the pillars is a peaceful experience in stark contrast to the relief carvings on tombs of saints known as 'the weepers', who are sculpted with emblems thought to be related to the manner of their martyrdom; one holds a chalice, another a saw, and another, thought to have been flayed, holds skin. A carving on another tomb shows St Margaret of Antioch conquering a dragon.

The abbey is a prime example of a medieval Cistercian abbey, awash with saintly figures and mythical creatures alike.

Above: An aerial view of the abbey.

Below: Medieval carvings.

49

25 Glasnevin Cemetery

Co. Dublin

Glasnevin Cemetery is not only the largest burial place in Ireland, it is also the first cemetery museum in the world. It was opened to the public in 1832, and is now the burial site of about 1.5 million people. Prior to the opening of the cemetery, Irish Catholics had no place of their own to bury their dead, with the Penal Laws restricting the public performance of services. Daniel O'Connell, founder of the Catholic Association, pushed for a place where both Catholics and Protestants could bury their dead with dignity. The cemetery is now home to O'Connell Tower, which commemorates him. Standing at 55 metres, it is the tallest round tower in Ireland.

The graves of a number of political figures and Irish artists can be found in Glasnevin Cemetery, including Éamon de Valera, Charles Stewart Parnell, Maude Gonne, Brendan Behan, and Luke Kelly. The most famous frequently visited grave, however, is probably that of revolutionary and politician Michael Collins.

There are also thought to be about 800,000 unmarked mass graves in the cemetery, holding the bodies of those who died in the Famine and the later cholera outbreak. The cemetery had areas dedicated to housing the bodies of those who died during certain epidemics, such as smallpox and typhoid. The grave in which the typhoid victims were buried was unwittingly located above an underground spring which actually contributed to the spread of the disease rather than containing it.

The insightful and varied tours offered in the cemetery tell the stories of not just the big names of Irish history, but also of the ordinary people who lived through it.

Sculpture of Mary holding the dying Jesus Christ, at Glasnevin Cemetery.

Leinster • Culture and Craic

26 Oratory of the Sacred Heart

Co. Dublin

The Oratory of the Sacred Heart, an unassuming building set back from a small street in Dún Laoghaire in Dublin, is a kaleidoscope of illustration. Beginning in 1920 to commemorate the end of the First World War, over 16 years every inch of the small chapel was hand-painted by Sister Concepta Lynch. Her breathtaking Celtic Revival art, featuring spirals, knots, and animals of all kinds, is complemented by stained glass windows by the Harry Clarke Studio.

27 Sean's Bar

Co. Westmeath

On the banks of the Shannon in Athlone, Sean's Bar is the oldest pub in Ireland – and might even be the oldest pub in the world. During renovations in the 1970s, it was discovered that one of the walls was made from wattle and wicker dating back to 900 AD. Still serving pints and hosting Irish music nights, it is a traditional Irish pub in the most traditional sense, having been in existence for over a thousand years.

Musicians in the bar.

Leinster • Culture and Craic

28 Francis Bacon's Studio

Co. Dublin

Born in Dublin in 1909, Francis Bacon lived between Ireland and England for much of his life. He settled in London in 1929 to work as an interior designer, and eventually went on to establish himself as one of the leading artists of his generation. His studio has been meticulously catalogued and preserved (including the dust!) and is on display in the Hugh Lane Gallery. It is beautiful chaos, giving an insight into the energetic mind of a great artist.

Francis Bacon's studio at the Hugh Lane Gallery.

29 National Gallery of Ireland

Co. Dublin

The National Gallery of Ireland opened its doors in January 1864 with a small collection of 112 pictures. Now, the national collection of Irish and European art has over 16,000 artworks, including oil paintings, prints, furniture, and sculpture. It holds regular exhibitions of internationally renowned artists, and attracts hundreds of thousands of visitors per year.

The building on Merrion Square in Dublin is itself a piece of architectural art. The original building was designed by Francis Fowke, an Irish engineer, and completed in 1864. The stunning Millennium Wing was added in the early 2000s, and the museum has since been renovated to preserve the historic complex.

The gallery's collection boasts art by Vermeer, Picasso, Rembrandt, and Monet. In 1993, the gallery was put on the world stage when Caravaggio's *The Taking of Christ*, a painting known through copies

The National Gallery of Ireland.

Leinster • Culture and Craic

but believed to have been destroyed, was discovered hanging in a Jesuit house of studies in Dublin. The painting is on loan to the gallery indefinitely by the Jesuits.

It also holds an annual J.M.W. Turner exhibition. The British art collector Henry Vaughan gave 31 of the artist's watercolours to the gallery with the request that they only be displayed in January to protect them from sunlight damage. The modern lighting techniques in the gallery mean this is now unnecessary, but they still honour Vaughan's request, and there is a Turner event every January.

The Irish artists in the collection include James Barry, Roderic O'Conor, Louis le Brocquy, and William Orpen. The gallery also has a Yeats Museum, showing the sketchbooks of Jack B. Yeats, which were donated by his niece, Irish painter Anne Butler Yeats, in 1996.

The National Gallery of Ireland was founded in response to the enthusiasm the Irish public displayed for art at an exhibition held on Leinster Lawn in Dublin in 1853, and in the spirit of its foundation, access to the gallery is free for all to enjoy.

William Orpen,
Looking at the Sea, 1912, at the
National Gallery of Ireland.

Natural Wonders

Bridges of Ross, Co. Clare.

Unique Ireland

The home of Irish coffee: Foynes Flying Boat & Maritime Museum, Co. Limerick.

The Great Outdoors

The Ring of Kerry, Co. Kerry.

Culture and Craic

The Guinness Cork Jazz Festival, Co. Cork.

30 Cliffs of Moher

Co. Clare

The awe-inspiring Cliffs of Moher were formed 320 million years ago. At their highest point, they are 214 metres, with a vertical cliff face that nose-dives into the ever-churning Atlantic. They run for about 14 kilometres, and there is a round stone tower at the midpoint of the cliffs known as O'Brien's Tower, named for Sir Cornelius O'Brien who built it in 1835. On a clear day, you can spot the Aran Islands in Galway Bay from the top of the tower.

The face of the cliffs mirrors the rolling waves that pelt it below, which have caused major erosion that has led to the formation of sea arches and stacks. A 67-metre sea stack called Branaunmore was once part of the cliffs, but the many layers of rock connecting it to the land were gnawed away by the ocean over time. The cliff rock is permeated with trace fossils, as well as worm trails and burrow holes of yet to be identified marine life.

The cliffs attract a staggering 1.5 million visitors a year, and you can walk an official path along the cliff top, where you will be humbled by the views and the force of the wind. There is also an unofficial path much closer to the edge, but walking this route wouldn't be wise.

Bird life is abundant on the cliffs at peak season, including razorbills and puffins. Grey seals, porpoises, basking sharks, and dolphins are among the sea life that visit the area. If you have a keen eye, you might also be able to spot a surfer braving the exhilarating and treacherous Aileen's Wave, one of the most famous of Ireland's big-wave surf spots off the Cliffs of Moher.

The beautiful Cliffs of Moher.

31 Skellig Michael

Co. Kerry

There is an otherworldly quality to Skellig Michael, a jagged pyramid of green off the coast of Kerry. It is one of two islands: the second, Little Skellig (or Sceilig Bheag) is inaccessible, while Skellig Michael gets around 11,000 visitors per year willing to brave the dicey landing at one of the island's harbours. The word 'Skellig' derives from the Irish 'sceilig', which can be translated as 'splinter of stone', and its first known mention appears in the Irish annals, which tell the story of a shipwreck around 1400 BC caused by the mythical Tuatha Dé Danann.

This otherworldly quality is amplified when you encounter the island's monastic settlement, which is thought to have been founded there in the 6th or 7th century. The distinctive beehive huts and monastery were built near the summit, on a terraced shelf 180 metres above sea level. These can only be reached by ascending the 618 craggy steps that wind up the body of the island, but the experience is transcendent. The difficulty in reaching the island due to unpredictable weather conditions means that it is remarkably intact, and walking among the ancient monastery is to feel like you're tracing the footsteps of the monks who lived in this impossible place centuries before.

Despite the inhospitable weather, the island is more ecologically diverse than the mainland. The Skelligs provide sanctuary to Ireland's largest gannet colony, as well as the eyries of peregrine falcons. However, it is encountering Skellig Michael's many puffins up close, busying themselves on the hillsides, that makes an already extraordinary experience nothing short of magical.

Skellig Michael, with Little Skellig in the background.

32 Bull Rock Island

Co. Cork

Bull Rock lies along the Beara Peninsula in Cork, just 4 kilometres from the larger and more well-known Dursey Island. It is one of three small islands in the area, the others called Cow Rock and Calf Rock. Bull Rock is off the beaten track and even though landing on the island isn't possible, the views from the boat are beyond impressive.

At 93 metres high, the island is small but intriguing. As you draw closer, you begin to see the outline of a building set into the rock face. This is an old two-storey building that housed generations of lighthouse keepers, and it looks as if it's being absorbed into the island. The original lighthouse was built in 1866 on Calf Rock, but it was destroyed years later when the tower snapped during a storm, leaving the lighthouse keepers trapped on the island for two weeks before they could be rescued. The lighthouse was eventually rebuilt on Bull Rock in 1889 and tended to by keepers, tasked with duties such as maintaining the lamp and cleaning the lenses, until it was replaced by an automated system in 1991.

The main attraction of the island, however, is the spectacular sea arch, a tunnel right through the island. This natural archway is known as the 'gateway to the Underworld', and if the tide allows, you can travel through the tunnel by boat. In Irish mythology, Tech Duinn, meaning 'House of Donn' (who is believed to be a god of the dead), is often associated with the eerie island of Bull Rock.

Bull Rock tunnel and lighthouse.

33 Bridges of Ross

Co. Clare

Once a trio of sea arches on the west side of Ross Bay, two of the bridges eroded over time and eventually crumbled into the water below. One bridge remains, and it is a beautiful geological phenomenon, with an archway of grass traversing the water below. It is accessible by a footpath, and you can spot the abundant birdlife as you stroll (carefully!) across the top.

Bridges of Ross, part of a rich coastal landscape.

Munster • Natural Wonders

34 Aillwee Cave

Co. Clare

First discovered in the 1940s by a farmer who followed his dog when it ran inside, Aillwee Cave holds calcite formations ranging between 8,000 and 350,000 years old. The cave wasn't explored until the 1970s when the farmer eventually told others of its existence, and the bones of brown bears were found, which were dated at over 10,000 years old. The cave also has a beautiful underground waterfall, which can be viewed by visitors along the 300-metre passage that's open to the public.

Aillwee Cave, discovered by Jack McGann while following his dog.

35 Doolin Cave

Co. Clare

Discovered in 1952 by a caving club and popular with spelunkers since, Doolin Cave was opened to the public in the 2000s after, controversially, the entrance was expanded to allow for visitors. The most famous feature of the 70-metre-deep cave is the Great Stalactite. It is one of the longest known free-hanging stalactites in the world, and was formed from continuous drops of water, a natural chandelier formed over thousands of years.

36 Irish Sky Garden

Co. Cork

The Irish Sky Garden in Skibbereen in Co. Cork is an art installation designed by American sculptor James Turrell, who is known for his large-scale pieces that play with light and space. It is on the grounds of the Liss Ard Estate, and was inspired by the neolithic ring fort from which the estate takes its name: 'Lios Ard' means 'high fort'. The photograph of the Sky Garden hardly does justice to what it is like to experience it.

Entering through an archway and megalithic-like passage, you ascend stairs to find yourself inside an oval-shaped grassy crater. In the centre lies a large stone plinth, similar in look to an Egyptian sarcophagus, upon which the visitor is to lie. From this perspective the elliptical crater is transformed, and you are entirely enveloped by grass walls that block intruding sounds, with the sky a blanket of light above – modern art intimately acquainted with timeless nature. Turrell said of the installation: 'The most important thing is that inside turns into outside and the other way around, in the sense that relationships between the Irish landscape and sky changes.'

Remarkably, the piece is unfinished, with the initial concept planning five separate constructions over 10 acres. Only one site was completed, but when the vastness of the sky is your canvas, it certainly seems like enough.

Munster • Unique Ireland

Visitors can lie on the stone to stare at the sky.

37 Poulnabrone Dolmen

Co. Clare

Out of the almost 200 dolmens in Ireland, Poulnabrone is one of the best known, and one of the most photographed. Dating from the Neolithic period, between 4200 BC and 2900 BC, it is a portal tomb, with a massive sloping capstone supported by standing stones on either side. The back stone, on the ground behind the tomb, appears to have fallen away at an unknown time. The capstone is four metres long and 30 centimetres thick, although it is still not the largest in Ireland – that title belongs to the capstone of Brownshill Dolmen in Co. Carlow, which is estimated to weigh over 100 tonnes.

It's not known how these enormous stones were raised to construct the portal tombs, but an excavation of the Poulnabrone site in the late 1980s has given us a fascinating insight into the lives of our Irish ancestors. The remains of approximately 33 people were found – men, women, and children. Only specific bones were buried at the dolmen, and evidence suggests that they had been stored elsewhere beforehand. Some bones showed scorch marks, meaning they may have been ritually burned before being placed beneath the earth. The bones show signs of hard labour, malnutrition, and infection, but they also show signs of violence: one hip bone is embedded with a flint arrowhead. Jewellery made from quartz crystal and bone was also found in the area.

It seems that the location was chosen for ritual, ceremony, or as a collective grave, but the mystery of why these specific bones of these specific people were buried at the imposing dolmen remains.

Munster • Unique Ireland

Poulnabrone Dolmen, photographed here at sunset, is a portal tomb located in the Burren, Co. Clare.

38 Foynes Flying Boat & Maritime Museum

Co. Limerick

The world's only flying boat museum is in Foynes in Co. Limerick, and it also happens to be where the Irish coffee was invented. This beautiful town on the River Shannon was a pivotal location in the aviation world in the 1930s and '40s. Fascinatingly, it was one of Europe's largest civilian airports during World War II. Transatlantic seaplanes, or 'flying boats', were a regular sight in the small village of Foynes, using the Shannon as their liquid runway.

Due to the town's strategic location on the western seaboard, it was the perfect location for an airport, and so a 19th-century hotel was converted into a terminal, with the control tower located at its highest point. This terminal has now been converted into a museum, displaying a full-size replica of a Boeing B314 flying boat, which you can walk around to enjoy a peek into the lavish world of 1940s jetsetters. VIP visitors to Foynes included John F. Kennedy, Eleanor Roosevelt, Ernest Hemingway, and Maureen O'Hara. O'Hara actually cut the ribbon at the opening of the museum in 1989.

Not just for aviation enthusiasts, the museum also tells the history of the Irish coffee, first made by chef Joe Sheridan, who ran the kitchen in the terminal's restaurant and coffee shop. The story is told that a flight bound for New York had to turn back to Foynes due to inclement weather, and so Sheridan prepared a warming beverage to welcome the American passengers on their return and lift their spirits.

Top: Full-size replica of a Boeing B314 flying boat.
Bottom: Enjoying an Irish coffee in the B314 cockpit.

Munster • Unique Ireland

39 Drombeg Stone Circle

Co. Cork

Known locally as the Druid's Altar, the circle is made of 17 standing stones, and appears to have been constructed to align with the sun on the winter solstice. During an excavation in the 1950s, a deliberately shattered pot holding cremated bones and wrapped in cloth was found at its centre. It isn't the most spectacular stone circle in existence, but it was found to be one of the most frequently used in Ireland, with radiocarbon dating showing activity between 1100 and 800 BC.

Drombeg stone circle.

Munster • Unique Ireland

40 The Metal Man
Co. Waterford

A cast-iron beacon overlooking Tramore in Co. Waterford, the Metal Man was constructed after HMS *Seahorse* sank when it became grounded at Brownstown Head in bad weather, resulting in the deaths of 360 people. This unusual beacon takes the shape of a man dressed in a blue jacket, a red top, and white trousers – the clothes of a Royal Navy petty officer. There is a matching statue at Rosses Point in Sligo Bay, and The Metal Man has even been depicted in paintings by Jack Butler Yeats.

Top: The Metal Man.
Bottom: Fossil tracks on Valentia island.

41 Tetrapod Trackway
Co. Kerry

These fossil tracks on Valentia Island, well-preserved by silt and transformed into rock, have been dated to be between 350 and 370 million years old. They are among the oldest evidence in the world of a four-legged vertebrate moving on land – significant because they eventually evolved into mammals and then into humans. The longest trackway shows as many as 145 imprints, and another shorter one shows evidence of a tail being dragged through the mud.

42 Burren National Park

Co. Clare

The vast, almost lunar-like landscape of the Burren appears in blunt contrast to the rolling green hills for which Ireland is known, but despite its barren appearance, the rock of the Burren is fertile. Among the mosaic of limestone pavement is a cornucopia of flora thriving in the Burren's complex ecosystem.

The Burren is a karst landscape, which means it formed from the dissolution of rocks such as limestone and dolomite. The limestone formed about 350 million years ago as sediment when a tropical sea covered most of Ireland. The compressed strata of this limestone contain fossilised corals and sea urchins.

The moon-like surface of the Burren.

Munster • The Great Outdoors

Over 70% of Ireland's flower species can be found in the Burren, protected within the gaps in the limestone, known as 'grikes'. Some species are even unique to the Burren. It is also home to many kinds of orchids and alpine plants, as well as moss and ferns -- a botanical paradise that is rarely out of bloom.

Fluttering among the colourful flowers is a wealth of butterfly and moth species, including the Burren Green moth, which can only be found in this area in Ireland. It is also one of the main breeding grounds in Ireland for the European pine marten, as well as being the territory of a host of feral goats.

Enjoy the singular landscape of the Burren by foot on the Burren Way, which takes about five days, or on a long, scenic drive.

43 Carrauntoohil

Co. Kerry

Located in the Iveragh Peninsula in Co. Kerry, Carrauntoohil is the highest mountain in Ireland at 1,039 metres, and it is the central peak in the MacGillycuddy's Reeks mountain range. It is a strenuous but rewarding hike, and definitely not one for beginners. The trails to the top take you to verdant valleys, quiet lakes, and craggy ridges, and the walk can take about six hours, depending on which route you choose.

There are three trails to reach the summit: the Devil's Ladder, Brother O'Shea's Gully, and Caher. Though its name is the most intimidating of the three, the Devil's Ladder is the most direct route, and therefore the most common. It's so popular that it's been nicknamed 'the tourist route' by frequent hikers. It gets its name from the intimidating steepness and loose rocks and pebbles that can make the trail a bit of a scramble at times. It's about 12 kilometres, and the path is easy to spot (in good weather!). The trail will take you across the stepping stones of the River Gaddagh, and to the gorgeous Hag's Glen with contrasting views of lake and valley.

The other routes are just as strenuous and even longer. One route via the Eagle's Nest will take you to Ireland's highest lake, Lough Cummeenoughter.

When you make it to the top of Carrauntoohil, you will be treated to panoramic views of Kerry, with the Gap of Dunloe to the east and Glencar to the west. There is a huge cross at the summit, where you can take a brief rest and revel in your achievement before you start the careful descent.

The view across Kerry.

44 Ring of Kerry

Co. Kerry

Making up 179 kilometres of meandering roads around the Iveragh Peninsula, with every turn on the Ring of Kerry you're met with a sight even more spectacular than the last: sparkling lakes, rushing rivers, sweeping hills, and rugged coastline. You'll be so bewitched by the scenery that you'll have no choice but to retreat to a nook in a cosy pub, have a nip of whiskey, and write a poem.

The journey starts in Killarney and takes about three and a half hours to drive if you don't stop, but with Moll's Gap, the Dunloe Ogham Stones, Rossbeigh Beach, Torc Waterfall, and Muckross Abbey among the many attractions along the way, you will be stretching your legs frequently. There is also an established walking path called the Kerry Way, and you can explore the scenic route by bicycle, which would be breathtaking in every sense of the word.

It is no doubt one of the most picturesque places in Ireland, and one of the most photographed. In fact, Ladies View, with its river carving through a sweeping green valley, was named thus because it was a favourite of Queen Victoria's ladies-in-waiting.

The route takes you through lots of charming towns, including Kenmare, Sneem, Waterville, and Portmagee, from where you can see the Skellig Islands off the coast. There are plenty of cafés and restaurants to stop and refresh, and you can enjoy seafood that's fresh off the boat. It's no wonder Kerry is known in Ireland as 'the Kingdom'.

Ladies View, Ring of Kerry.

45 Waterford Greenway

Co. Waterford

Stretching from Waterford city to the picturesque harbour town of Dungarvan, the greenway extends to 46 kilometres and is completely car-free. As it makes use of a disused railway, the terrain is mostly flat, so most people choose to cycle the trail, though you are free to walk or run it if you like. The greenway takes you across viaducts, through tunnels, and past the foothills of the Comeragh Mountains, with medieval ruins, Norman castles, and old railway stations to see along the way.

A dusk-time view of the historic city of Waterford.

Above: Kilmacthomas Viaduct, part of the Waterford Greenway.

Muckross House.

46 Killarney National Park

Co. Kerry

The first national park in Ireland, Killarney National Park extends to over 100 square kilometres of lakes, woodlands, and mountains. Among the uplands of the park, in the Torc and Mangerton mountains, is Ireland's only herd of red deer, as well as rare bird species including merlins, osprey, and peregrine falcons. At the heart of the wildness of the park are the manicured gardens of Muckross House, a 19th-century mansion.

Left: Bus and truck drivers are warned not to venture into the Conor Pass.
Below: The road is very narrow, even for cars.

47 Conor Pass

Co. Kerry

This serpentine road is one of the highest mountain passes in Ireland, taking you up and up until the cliff face hugs you on one side and the mountain plummets away on the other. It can be nerve-wracking, with space for only one car to pass at the narrowest sections, but the views from the top are breathtaking. As well as the sublime landscape, you can see the vibrant town of Dingle below, where you can soon calm your nerves with a pint in Dick Mack's pub.

48 Adare Manor

Co. Limerick

An ornate and grand house on the banks of the River Maigue, Adare Manor's known history goes back as far as 1226, following the Norman invasion of Ireland, when King Henry III granted an eight-day fair to be held there following the Feast of St James. From then, it passed through a succession of earls, including the Earls of Kildare and Desmond, but the person who built the manor as we know it today was Windham Henry Quin, the 2nd Earl of Dunraven.

The Earl was fond of the outdoors, but had been confined to the house due to a crippling case of gout. His wife, Lady Caroline Dunraven, encouraged him to spend his time designing a spectacular home for them. And so, in the early 1830s, the Earl of Dunraven's architectural remodel began. The transformation was lavish, with the best of craftsmanship on display in the stained-glass windows, wood carvings, tiled fireplaces, intricate stonework, and labyrinthine gardens. The time spent by the Earl on the design is reflected in the detail – it is a calendar house, with 365 leaded windows, 52 chimneys, and 4 towers to mark the days, weeks, and seasons in a year.

The work, as well as being exquisite, provided much-needed income for the people of the surrounding areas during the Great Famine. Lady Caroline, too, wanted to create employment opportunities for the local women and so she established a school of embroidery.

Munster • Culture and Craic

84

Adare Manor is now a luxury hotel, though the work of the Dunravens is still there in all its beauty and extravagance, including the carved words from the Bible along the top of the building that read: 'Except the Lord build the house, their labour is but lost that build it.'

Right: Windham Quin, 2nd Earl of Dunraven and Mount-Earl.
Below: Adare Manor, Co. Limerick.

49 Spike Island

Co. Cork

Inhabited in turn by monks, pirates, soldiers, and prisoners, the history of Spike Island is a storied one. In the 7th century, Saint Mochuda founded a monastery on the island, and it was the territory of the monks for centuries before the Vikings invaded Ireland. The location of the island, while likely attractive to monks for its solitude, became a place of military operation in 1779 when work on a British army fortress began. The towering walls, hidden tunnels, and clever star-shaped building of the 24-acre Fort Mitchel were characteristics of the cutting-edge military design employed to defend Cork Harbour, which could shelter entire fleets. Over a century later, Winston Churchill drew attention to Spike Island's strategic location by calling it one of the 'sentinel towers of the approaches to Western Europe'.

The huge fortress, which could fit the entire of Alcatraz Island inside it, was then used as an island prison. In fact, it grew to be the largest prison in the British Empire in the 1850s, packing over 2,300 people inside its walls, many of whom were convicted for stealing in a famine-stricken Ireland. It even had a children's prison, where boys as young as 11 were held. The conditions were terrible, and 1,300 people died and were buried there in unmarked mass graves.

The dark history of Spike Island didn't end there, with the fortress being used as a prison again during the Irish War of Independence, housing IRA prisoners. Seven of these prisoners escaped through a hole in the wall during the truce of 1921. The island was eventually ceded to Ireland as part of the Anglo-Irish Trade Agreement in 1938.

Munster • Culture and Craic

Remarkably, the island continued to be used as a prison, with an infamous riot in 1985, until it closed in 2004. It is now a heritage tourist site, just a 15-minute boat journey from the harbour town of Cobh.

Bird's eye view of Fort Mitchel on Spike Island.

50 The Butter Museum

Co. Cork

Butter is one of Ireland's most important exports, and its production provides a unique, if creamy, lens through which to view the social, domestic, and economic history of the country. The Cork Butter Museum is located in the building that housed the historic Cork Butter Market, dating from 1849, in the Shandon area of Cork city. Shandon was the location of Ireland's largest open-air butchery, called a 'Shambles', where the butter was traded.

Ireland's weather ensures that large amounts of grass can be grown over a long season, meaning the dairy industry could flourish, with butter from grass-fed cows still in huge demand. The export market of Irish butter started to take off in the 1700s, and the Cork Butter Market became the largest butter exchange in the world by the 1800s. Irish butter travelled globally, and made it to the far reaches of the Caribbean, India, and Australia.

The craft of butter-making is a long-standing one in Ireland. Preserving butter in bogs was a common practice, and the museum has a keg of 1,000-year-old bog butter on display. The collection also showcases paraphernalia such as old milk churns, a collection of butter wrappers, and firkins or barrels, which were used by farmers to transport their butter. The exhibit gives unique insight into domestic dairy cattle farming, butter production and trade, and it includes a section about Kerrygold, Ireland's most famous brand of butter, the commercial success of which means that Irish butter is still making its way to households across the globe.

Munster • Culture and Craic

Above: Cork Butter Museum exhibits.

Below: Home of the museum in the former Cork Butter Market.

51 King John's Castle

Co. Limerick

One of the best-preserved Norman castles in Europe is at the centre of Limerick's medieval quarter. Its 13th-century walls were damaged during the 1642 Siege of Limerick – the first of five sieges on the city – when Irish Confederate troops took the castle from an English garrison. Now the great walls and towers of the castle loom over the River Shannon and remain an iconic landmark in the heart of Limerick City.

52 The Rock of Cashel

Co. Tipperary

The Rock of Cashel was the original seat of the High Kings of Munster. Its location on an outcrop, the ancient buildings erupting from the surrounding green hills, lends to its dramatic air. The legendary Brian Boru was crowned High King there in the late 900s. Few of the early buildings have survived, with the majority of those existing today dating from the 12th and 13th centuries, though Cormac's Chapel contains the only survivng Romanesque frescoes in Ireland.

Below: Aerial view of the Rock of Cashel, circa 1970, prior to any modern work.

Opposite: The castle, showing the defensive walls.

Munster • Culture and Craic

92

53 Guinness Cork Jazz Festival

Co. Cork

Established in 1978, the Guinness Cork Jazz Festival is a stalwart in Ireland's music scene, attracting tens of thousands every October. Performers have included legends such as Ella Fitzgerald and B.B. King, with Mack Fleetwood and Corinne Bailey Rae recently gracing the stages. Brass bands move through the streets of Cork making the city vibrate, while jazz purists can enjoy world-renowned musicians in different venues.

Below: Chicago band Hypnotic Brass Ensemble play at the Cork Opera House during the festival.

Opposite: Macy Gray performing at the Cork Opera House.

Munster • Culture and Craic

Natural Wonders

Benbulben, with Classiebawn Castle in the foreground, Co. Sligo.

Unique Ireland

The Deserted Village at Slievemore provides a haunting reminder of times past, Co. Mayo.

The Great Outdoors

Connemara National Park, Co. Galway.

Culture and Craic

Galway's famous Oyster & Seafood Festival, Co. Galway.

54 Cave of the Cats

Co. Roscommon

This narrow, 37-metre cave in Roscommon is an ordinary geological formation with an extraordinary mythological connection. This natural fissure in the limestone which covers the area is called Oweynagat (Uaimh na gCat), or Cave of the Cats, and was known in the distant past as 'Ireland's Gate to Hell'.

It has a strong relationship with Samhain, when the veil between this world and the Otherworld is believed to be at its thinnest, allowing spirits to walk between the two – and the Cave of the Cats is their exit. As such, Roscommon is often thought to be the birthplace of Halloween.

In the medieval period, a souterrain (a type of underground gallery) was constructed at the natural cave entrance. This included two Ogham stones acting as lintels, one of which is inscribed with words that roughly translate as '[The Stone of] Fróech, son of Medb'. Queen Medb is one of the main characters in the Ulster Cycle (a body of medieval Irish heroic legends), with her palace thought to have been in the surrounding Rathcroghan. Other myths tell of The Morrígan, an Irish battle goddess, who is said to have emerged from Oweynagat on a chariot pulled by a one-legged chestnut horse.

The tales of Ireland's rich and exhilarating mythology are deeply entwined with the landscape here. They have made a simple cave, which on first glance looks like a ditch, much more than stone and earth. The natural geological formation of the Cave of the Cats takes on a power of epic proportions, and has undeniable cultural significance.

Connacht • Natural Wonders

The entrance to Oweynagat, the Cave of the Cats.
A place of contact between this world and the
Otherworld, especially at Samhain, or Halloween.

55 Benbulben

Co. Sligo

The distinct formation of Benbulben was shaped by glaciers during the Ice Age. It is a 'table mountain', with steep sides climbing to a flat surface. It's the most recognisable peak in the Dartry Mountains, and it can be seen from a distance, shooting up from the surrounding green fields, the ever-recognisable pointed side giving it the look of the bow of a ship.

The name 'Benbulben' (also spelled Ben Bulben and Benbulbin) comes from the Irish 'Binn Ghulbain', with 'Binn' meaning 'peak' or 'mountain' and 'Ghulbain' possibly meaning 'beak' or 'jaw'. The mountain rocks were formed about 330 million years ago when much of the area was a shallow sea. In fact, though it is fully on land, it contains fossilised sea shells and corals. The mountain is made up

Connacht • Natural Wonders

of limestone on top of shaly mudstone, the discrete layers adding to its unmistakable appearance.

Among the plants that can be found on Benbulben are many of an Arctic–alpine variety, which flourish due to the cooler temperature at the top of the mountain. Fringed sandwort, an unimposing flower with delicate white petals, has been there since before the last ice age, and the plant species may well be over 100,000 years old.

The mountain is located in an area known as Yeats' Country, named for the Irish poet W.B. Yeats who wrote about the mountain affectionately in 'Under Ben Bulben': 'Under bare Ben Bulben's head/ In Drumcliff churchyard Yeats is laid.' He got his wish, and his grave can be visited in the nearby Drumcliff Cemetery, though he was first buried in France and not reinterred in Sligo, with some difficulty, until nine years after his death.

The majestic Benbulben.

56 Dún Briste Sea Stack

Co. Mayo

The 45-metre-tall Dún Briste sea stack was once part of the mainland, and legend has it that St Patrick struck the ground with his crozier, causing the rock to break away. The more scientifically minded believe that it was once connected by a sea arch that collapsed during a raging storm in 1393. In fact, 'Dún Briste' translates from Irish as 'Broken Fort'.

Located just a short distance from land, the stack feels almost touchable. The layers upon layers of rock that comprise the sea stack are clearly visible, with their jagged edges and different colours making it a thing of beauty. It has a grassy top that is the exclusive territory of nesting birds, such as puffins, cormorants, and kittiwakes.

In 1981, a team including an archaeologist landed on the sea stack by helicopter to study it, and they found two stone buildings and an opening in a wall that was used in medieval times to allow sheep to pass from one field to another. The rock, so attractive in its proximity to the land, has also been tackled by climbers a few times in recent history.

Opposite: Dún Briste sea stack.
Below: The '64 Eire' sign.

Just inland from the sea stack on Downpatrick Head you can find a large blowhole, where you can gaze down into the water and witness the unstoppable waves of the Atlantic. On a stormy day, spray shoots up through the hole. The headland was also the site of a look-out post during World War II, and you can still see a huge sign embedded in the land reading '64 EIRE', which indicated to aircraft that they were in neutral Ireland.

Connacht • Natural Wonders

57 Doolough Pass

Co. Mayo

Between Mweelrea mountain and Sheeffry Hills, the Doolough Pass is wild and beautiful. It overlooks Doolough (which translates from Irish as 'black lake') and the surrounding valley. It is also the site of a famine memorial. A stone cross commemorates the 1849 tragedy when many people perished from exposure and malnutrition on their way to report at an old hunting lodge so that they could keep receiving 'outdoor relief', a form of social welfare.

58 Glencar Waterfall

Co. Leitrim

Reached by a short but scenic wooded walk, the Glencar Waterfall is a modest 15 metres high, but its beauty is unmatched. Its sheets of water fall among the lush foliage of the encroaching trees, and you can swim in nearby Glencar Lake, with caution. The waterfall is so beautiful that it served as inspiration for W.B. Yeats, who mentioned it in the third verse of his poem 'The Stolen Child'.

Where the wandering water gushes

From the hills above Glen-Car,

In pools among the rushes

That scarce could bathe a star,

We seek for slumbering trout

And whispering in their ears

Give them unquiet dreams;

Leaning softly out

From ferns that drop their tears

Over the young streams.

Come away, O human child!

To the waters and the wild

With a faery, hand in hand,

For the world's more full of weeping than you can understand.

The waterfall tumbling through the trees.

59 Aasleagh Falls

Co. Mayo

In Mayo, near the border with Galway, this wide waterfall on the Erriff River is small but powerful. The falls are open, unencumbered by the adjacent woods, with a small green hill on the opposite side that's perfect for a picnic while you listen to the water spill over the ledge. You can also cross the Aasleagh Falls Bridge to take in the views of the falls and watch people fishing for salmon in this popular spot.

Opposite: Two fish jumping at Aasleagh Falls, Erriff River, Mayo.

Below: Aasleagh Falls on Erriff River with a single house under Letterass Mountains with a dark and dramatic sky in the background.

Connacht • Natural Wonders

60 Harry Clarke Stained Glass, Ballinrobe

Co. Mayo

The stained glass of Harry Clarke is instantly recognisable for its jewel tones, detailed figures, and the clever integration of the window leading in the design. The art is astonishing in its beauty, and we are lucky that a lot of it can be viewed in public places around Ireland. The most extensive collection is in St Mary's Church in Ballinrobe, and includes eight double-light windows, 16 panels in all, which were commissioned by Monsignor D'Alton in 1924. The first four windows depict events in the lives of Jesus and the Virgin Mary. The second four windows show a series of images of Irish saints. The colours are rich, the backgrounds are abstract, and the faces and clothing of each figure are ornate – all incredible when you consider the delicate medium through which Clarke worked.

Harry Clarke apprenticed in the studio of his father, a church decorator, and attended evening classes in the Metropolitan College of Art and Design. He also worked as a book illustrator, and he was picked up by Harrap Publishers, eventually illustrating a number of books for them, though some of his drawings for those projects were lost during the 1916 Rising. He died prematurely at the age of 41 from tuberculosis, having completed over 130 stained-glass windows in his short life along with his brother Walter. Some of his work is on display in the Hugh Lane Gallery, though most are still where they were intended to be – with light dancing through them as you sip a coffee in Bewley's on Grafton Street in Dublin, or as you stop for a moment of contemplation in a church.

Three of the panels at St Mary's Church.

61 Céide Fields

Co. Mayo

Buried beneath a blanket bog in Co. Mayo is the oldest known stone-walled field system in the world. The Céide Fields are 6,000 years old – predating the pyramids by about 2,000 years – and comprise a system of fields, dwellings, and megalithic tombs. There is estimated to be about 100 kilometres of stone walls beneath the natural peat bog, which developed there over thousands of years and has its own unique vegetation.

The Neolithic site was first happened upon in the 1930s when a local school teacher, Patrick Caulfield, was cutting peat for fuel. He kept unearthing piles of stones, which were abundant and of a similar depth, making him realise that they must have been placed there by earlier settlers. However, it wasn't until his son Seamus, a

Connacht • Unique Ireland

trained archaeologist, began investigating the site 40 years later that the extent and intricacy of the settlement was discovered. The walls were mapped by inserting iron probes into the bog to trace the walls, a method that would preserve the site.

The excavation unearthed details about the community who created this now-submerged system. They were likely farmers who cleared a pine and birch woodland to grow crops and rear cattle. Evidence also suggests that the climate was warmer back then, providing ideal growing conditions. The visitor centre, made from durable natural materials to complement the environment, has an exhibit that includes a 4,300-year-old Scots pine, beautifully preserved by the bog. It also has an indoor and outdoor viewing platform, providing sweeping views of both the fields and the Atlantic from its clifftop location.

A panoramic view of the bog landscape and megalithic site at the Céide Fields.

62 Benbulben Baryte Mine

Co. Sligo

In the depths of Benbulben, part of the Dartry Mountains, there is an abandoned baryte mine. The underground system of caves was populated with miners for over 80 years until it closed in the 1960s. Locals climbed the mountain daily to descend to this busy subterranean location, with the complex mine system including hostels and break rooms among ore crushers and dynamite storage rooms. Now the tunnels and vertical shafts echo with eerie abandonment, the remains of the ladders and lift system rusty with disuse.

Baryte is a non-metallic ore that's used widely as a filler or extender. It's used in oil and gas exploration mining, as well as in paint, paper, and the sugar-refining process. The mine in Benbulben was a prime resource for the mineral, though its location in the mountains was undoubtedly tricky to reach.

The baryte was transported down the mountain towards Glencar Lake by a cable-car system, and the pylon and wire ropes can still be seen on the mountain, ghosts of the clever engineering it took to excavate baryte from this limestone-rich mountain. Nature has worked its way into the mine, though much of the structure remains, albeit in a decayed state.

As well as having to climb the mountain to reach the mine, it is a dangerous place to explore, with specialist equipment needed to reduce the risk. However, you can hike the Glencar escarpment, with its glacial valley, waterfall, and lake, and pass the Benbulben mine en route, which remains an artefact of industry surrounded by nature's riches.

The Gleniff Valley Mine Track on Benbulben, site of a deep cavern where baryte was extracted.
(Please note: the mine access track is on private property.)

63 Dún Aonghasa

Co. Galway

Perched on a cliff on Inis Mór, hugging the Atlantic Ocean, Dún Aonghasa is the largest of the stone forts on the Aran Islands. It is thought to be about 3,000 years old, though little is known about the 'Aonghasa' who gives it its name. It is made of four concentric walled semicircles, with a platformed enclosure that is exposed to the buffeting winds of the coastline and a 100-metre drop to the crashing water below.

Below: Dún Aonghasa, the largest prehistoric stone fort on Inis Mór in the Aran Islands.

Opposite: A closer view of the fort, showing the sheer drop to the sea.

64 Medb's Cairn

Co. Sligo

At the summit of Knocknarea, a large hill in Co. Sligo, is a huge 5,000-year-old cairn comprising thousands of loose stones. It has not been excavated, so who is buried there and why is still a mystery. However, it is known as Medb's Cairn, as the mythological queen of Connacht is rumoured to have been buried here. There are other cairns, much less intact, dotted around Knocknarea, though it is the prominence of Medb's Cairn that has elevated this simple hill into a monument.

Left: Queen Medb by J. C. Leyendecker, Medb is queen of Connacht in the Ulster Cycle of Irish mythology.

Opposite: Snow falls on Medb's Cairn.

Connacht • Unique Ireland

65 Slievemore Deserted Stone Village

Co. Mayo

The remnants of almost 100 stone cottages stand at the foot of Slievemore mountain on Achill Island. These are the ghosts of a booley village, which was occupied during the summer months to provide cattle with fresh grazing ground. The act of 'booleying' – moving between locations depending on the season – continued on Achill long after the rest of Ireland turned to permanent settlement. The village was abandoned after the Great Famine, although some are thought to have still been used seasonally well into the 20th century.

Beautiful view at dusk of Slievemore mountain in Silver Strand, Achill Island.

Abandoned dry stone cottage in the deserted
village of Slievemore in Achill Island.

66 Aran Islands

Co. Galway

The windy and wild Aran Islands lie off the coast of Galway, comprising three islands in all: Inis Mór, Inis Meáin, and Inis Oírr. Together they make up only 46 square kilometres; Inis Mór, as the name suggests ('mór' meaning 'big' in Irish), is the largest of the three and the most visited. It has a population of about 800 people and there's a lot packed into this small island.

The best way to explore Inis Mór is by bicycle, though the weather can sometimes provide a challenge. There's the 3,000-year-old Dún Aonghasa fort sitting right against a cliff edge, and the soft sands and

Cottages at Killeany on Inis Mór, Aran Islands.

Abandoned thatched cottage on Inis Mór, Aran Islands.

clear water of Kilmurvey Beach, where you can dip your toes in the Atlantic if conditions are safe and you can manage the temperature. There's also Seal Colony Viewpoint, which is exactly as it sounds. Here, particularly at low tide, you can spot seals taking a rest on the rocks.

While Inis Meáin and Inis Oírr are much smaller, they are equally rugged and gorgeous, with turquoise waters, fishing boats, bracing winds, and pubs for a much-needed pint after exploring the islands. All islands are covered in stone walls, constructed without mortar over generations to create arable land on the rocky, weather-beaten landscape. They are ubiquitous, and they create a beautiful pattern of grey and green as you stroll or cycle around the islands.

The Aran Islands are Gaeltacht areas, with the first language of the locals being a beautiful Connemara Irish. The preservation of the Irish language is a testament to the tenacity and elegance of island life – and only a 40-minute boat journey from Galway.

67 Lough Key Forest Park

Co. Roscommon

Lough Key Forest Park is an 800-acre park on the shores of Lough Key in Co. Roscommon. The forested area of the park has evergreen, deciduous, and huge cedar trees, which can be uniquely viewed from the park's tree canopy walk, rising nine metres above the forest floor. There are plenty of wild flowers and wildlife, and the lake is dotted with small islands that can be explored by boat.

As well as the natural wonders of the area, the estate of Lough Key is of historical interest. Back as far as the 12th century, the park was known as Moylurg, which was then ruled by the McDermotts. Their residence was on one of the lake's islands, now known as Castle Island. The McDermotts ruled the area until the estate was granted to the King family in the 17th century during

the Cromwellian settlements, and they renamed it Rockingham. The Kings built a mansion in the park, which was eventually destroyed, but the tunnels underneath leading to the lake, made to hide the servants from view, remain and can be explored. Moylurg Viewing Tower was built on the site of the old mansion in the 1970s, its brutalist architecture style sticking out like a sore thumb in its natural, though cultivated, surroundings.

There are traffic-free cycle trails and a number of way-marked walking routes in the park, taking you past follies, bridges, and canals. There are also stables, ringforts, a deer paddock, church ruins, a fairy bridge, and a wishing chair. The park is a popular destination for visitors, particularly families, and you can make the most of the outdoors by camping onsite.

McDermott's Castle on Castle Island, Lough Key Forest Park. The 12th century building sits on a small island in the middle of the lake and is a national monument.

68 Croagh Patrick

Co. Mayo

Croagh Patrick stands 764 metres above Clew Bay in Co. Mayo. Its conical-shaped peak, once reached, rewards climbers with panoramic views of the drumlins of Clew Bay, the surrounding mountains, and the town of Westport. It is an iconic location and considered Ireland's 'holiest' mountain.

The history of this mountain as a place of ritual is thought to stretch as far back as the pagans, over 3,000 years ago, when people climbed the mountain to celebrate the beginning of harvest. Archaeological surveys found evidence of an enclosure at the mountaintop, along with dozens of circular huts adjacent to it. Its current name, however, has a Christian association, with the Irish name 'Cruach Phádraig' translating as 'Patrick's Stack'. St Patrick is said to have spent 40 days fasting at the summit of the mountain in 441 AD.

There has been a church at the summit since the 5th century, with the current modern church still hosting masses on days of pilgrimage. The mountain is known colloquially as 'The Reek', and it is tradition to climb it on Reek Sunday, the last Sunday of July, with around 25,000 people making the journey every year. Some pilgrims have done the climb barefoot, and it is not an easy one even with sturdy boots and a walking stick. It is a relentless ascent, with a difficult section of loose stones towards the top, which can provide an even bigger challenge on the way down. The weather, too, is likely to change while on the mountain, and the ascent and descent can take up to four hours.

Above: Chapel on the summit of Croagh Patrick and warning notice on the path.

Below: Croagh Patrick seen from Louisburgh.

69 Keem Beach

Co. Mayo

This horseshoe-shaped beach on Achill Island is perfect for swimming in summer months and for leisurely strolls when it's colder, with shelter from the elements provided by Croaghaun Mountain. It's a Blue Flag beach, one of five on Achill, and its clear, aquamarine waters reflect its quality. Basking sharks and dolphins can be spotted in the waters, while sheep can often be seen grazing on the nearby hillsides. There's a perfect view of the beach on the drive down from the clifftop, and there is a short yet spectacular walk along the cliffs of Benmore towards Achill Head.

The wide sweep of Keem Beach.

Connacht • The Great Outdoors

Stone bridge in the Great Western Greenway.

70 Great Western Greenway

Co. Mayo

The Great Western Greenway – Ireland's first greenway – follows
the old Midlands Great Western Railway, so its minor gradients
are perfect for a walking and cycling trail. It is 49 kilometres in all,
starting in Westport and on to Achill Sound, with an extension to
Cashel added in 2023. The traffic-free route takes you past woodlands,
coastline, bogs, mountains, and farmland, and you can stop along
the way for a bite to eat in the charming villages of Newport and
Mulranny before heading off again to take in more of the scenery.

71 Connemara National Park

Co. Galway

A lot of the 2,000-hectare Connemara National Park used to be part of the Kylemore Abbey Estate, but it is now owned by the state and is a sensational place to explore. There are plenty of walking trails that meander through the park's unique habitats, or you can go for a more challenging hike up one of the mountains that are part of the famous Twelve Bens. If you're lucky, you might even encounter a friendly Connemara pony along the way.

Below: A Connemara pony in the national park. *Opposite:* The stunning view out to sea.

72 Kylemore Abbey

Co. Galway

Nestled between a mountain and a lake in Pollacappul in Galway is the luxurious Kylemore Abbey, its light-grey stone distinct among its leafy surroundings. Yet somehow it feels like this palatial building is a natural part of the environment.

The mansion was built in 1867 by Mitchell Henry, a successful businessman, as a token of love for his wife, Margaret, who had become enchanted with the location while visiting on their honeymoon. It took four years to complete and contains an extravagant 33 bedrooms, four sitting rooms, a ballroom, and a library, among many other features. Henry and his wife lived there with their children until his wife tragically died only a few years after the building was completed. devastated by the loss, life for Henry in Kylemore Abbey was never the same.

The house was later sold, and it eventually passed into the hands of Benedictine Nuns who had fled the continent during World War I. They opened Kylemore Abbey as a school for girls, and the building has remained a monastery since the nuns took over in 1920. It is now under The Kylemore Trust and is a leading visitor attraction. There is a large Victorian walled garden within the estate, interestingly in the middle of a bog, featuring a flower garden, vegetable garden, fruit trees, and rockery, and only plants and flowers that grew during Victorian times are planted there today. The estate also contains other buildings, such as a Gothic chapel and mausoleum, where Mitchell and Margaret Henry are interred, still together in the little piece of Connemara they carved out for themselves over a century ago.

Above: Margaret Henry (1829–1874). Opposite: A scenic view of Kylemore Abbey in autumn.

Connacht • Culture and Craic

73 MV *Plassy*, Inis Oírr

Co. Galway

The MV *Plassy*, now rusted and stranded on the rocks of Inis Oírr, was bought in 1951 by Limerick Steamship Company Limited and sailed its cargo as far as Russia and South Africa. But it was off the coast of Inis Oírr in Galway that the ship ran into trouble.

In March 1960, en route from Fenit in Kerry to Galway with a cargo of stained glass, whiskey, and yarn, among other things, the *Plassy* was caught in a raging storm. Valentia Radio Station was broadcasting gale force 8 to 9, and the *Plassy* got the brunt of it. The storm's furious winds and monstrous waves ran it onto Finnis Rock – a flat limestone plateau hardly visible in the dim light. One crew member, Eddie Reidy, said that the ship hit the rock so forcefully that he was 'taken off the deck and hit the ceiling'.

Stranded due to the dangerous sea conditions, they sent a distress call and word got to the Life Saving Service. They would attempt to rescue the 11 crew members using the breeches buoy, a rope-based rescue device used to extract people from wrecked vessels. Thankfully, some locals were trained in its use, though it had never been deployed on Inis Oírr before. A crowd of islanders turned up to help in the rescue, and all crew members were delivered safely to shore. They had to remain on the island for a few days due to the weather conditions, but they were well looked after by the locals.

A few weeks later, the remaining cargo and other materials were salvaged by locals, with the ship boardable during low tide. The *Plassy* was driven further and further onshore over the following years due to storms and tides, and remains there as a memorial to the lives rescued that day.

The *Plassy* shipwreck at Inis Oírr.

74 Brigit's Garden

Co. Galway

Brigit's Garden in Rosscahill, Co. Galway, is laid out to reflect the cycle of the year, with the Celtic festivals of Samhain, Imbolc, Bealtaine, and Lughnasa marking each season. The garden covers 11 acres of native woodland and wildflower meadows, with the Calendar Sundial, which uses ancient techniques and a five-foot spear of bog oak to tell both the time of day and month of the year, a magnificent centrepiece.

Wildflowers by the Roundhouse.

The beautiful Samhain garden.

Connacht • Culture and Craic

136

75 Macnas Halloween Parade

Co. Galway

Macnas, an award-winning theatre company, showcase their considerable talent in this spectacular Halloween parade. Their production team, professional artists, and hundreds of volunteers put together a parade that tens of thousands of spectators gather to marvel at in Galway each year. The immersive performances feature dancers, musicians, and puppeteers, with original occult themes and stories inspired by mythology the perfect way to celebrate Halloween in its birthplace of Ireland.

A scene with a huge puppet at Macnas Halloween parade at Salmon Weir Bridge.

76 Galway Oyster & Seafood Festival

Co. Galway

The Galway Oyster & Seafood Festival is the oldest oyster festival in the world. It was started in 1954 by Brian Collins, a hotel manager, to try to entice visitors to the county during the quieter month of September. With just 34 guests in its first year, it is now internationally recognised. The festival is held at the beginning of oyster season, on the last week of September every year, and showcases native Galway oysters, as well as attracting competitors from all over the world to compete in the Oyster Opening Championships.

A parade through the streets during the festival.

Connacht • Culture and Craic

Left: A competitor shucks an oyster at the festival.

Below: Ready to begin the competition.

Natural Wonders

The magic of a becalmed Lough Neagh, spanning counties Antrim, Down, Armagh, Tyrone and Derry-Londonderry, is just one of many such places in Ulster.

Unique Ireland

Find out about the sinking of the unsinkable ship at the *Titanic* Museum in Belfast.

The Great Outdoors

The mysterious Navan Fort, Co. Armagh.

Culture and Craic

Discover the oldest licenced distillery in the world at Bushmills, Co. Antrim.

77 Giant's Causeway

Co. Antrim

Tucked into an arc at the base of soaring cliffs on the Co. Antrim coast, the Giant's Causeway is a UNESCO World Heritage Site and one of the most visited places in Northern Ireland. The Causeway is made up of about 40,000 basalt columns, formed over 50 million years ago when the area experienced powerful volcanic activity. The molten basalt burst through a fissure, rapidly cooling to form the unique pillars, some of which are 12 metres high. Most are hexagonal in shape, though some have seven or eight sides. The interlocking pattern of the pillars gives this natural geological formation an otherworldly appearance.

The columns form stepping stones that disappear into the sea, and they have a matching set across the water on the Scottish isle of Staffa, which inspired a famous Irish legend. Fionn mac Cumhaill, an Irish mythological hero, was challenged to a fight by the Scottish giant Benandonner, and Fionn built the Giant's Causeway so they could meet. However, legend has it that Fionn was worried Benandonner was too big to defeat, so his wife, Sadhbh, hatched a plan. She disguised Fionn as a baby, and when Benandonner reached Ireland and saw this massive infant, he assumed the baby's father, Fionn, must be gargantuan. Shaken, Benandonner fled back to Scotland, ripping up the columns of the Causeway behind him along the way so Fionn couldn't give chase.

The Giant's Causeway, in its distinctive beauty, certainly lives up to the legend. You can make the experience even more unique by arriving via the Bushmills Railway on a historic tramway. You can also arrive by foot along the Causeway Coast Way, a breathtaking 52 kilometre stretch of Ireland's coastline.

Atlantic waves break over the Giant's Causeway.

Ulster • Natural Wonders

78 Marble Arch Caves

Co. Fermanagh

The Marble Arch Caves in Co. Fermanagh were formed over 340 million years ago, and they lay unexplored until 1895 when Édouard-Alfred Martel and Lyster Jameson entered the cave by canvas boat, with only candlelight and magnesium flares to light their way. They were met by colossal chambers, sinkholes, and an underground river, and they discovered only 300 metres of the 11.5-kilometre system. Further exploration of the cave was carried out in the early 1900s by a group of English cavers from the Yorkshire Ramblers' Club, and speleologists (scientists who study caves) were able to map the cave more extensively in the 1960s due to advancements in cave diving.

The cave is now considered the longest known system in Northern Ireland, as well as being one of the most popular river show-caves in Ireland and the UK. It was formed by three rivers trickling down from Cuilcagh Mountain, which merge underground to form the Cladagh. Years of erosion have created this limestone labyrinth, and the cave continues to evolve due to the river rushing through it. The name Marble Arch is taken from a nearby limestone archway, another creation of time and erosion, which has been so polished by water that its shiny surface has the appearance of marble.

Development of the current show-cave began in 1982, and the candlelight first used to survey the cave has been replaced by soft electric lighting so that modern visitors can view the many calcite formations, cavernous roofs, and cave curtains. An electric flat-bottomed boat takes you along the subterranean river, and a purpose-built walkway allows visitors to explore the cave safely, including a short section called the Moses Walk, where the river runs along either side of the path at shoulder level.

The river inside the cave.

79 Ring of Gullion

Co. Armagh

The Ring of Gullion in Armagh is a group of volcanic hills that have eroded over time, forming a ring shape with Slieve Gullion at the centre. It was the first ring dyke to be mapped, and it has been named an Area of Outstanding Natural Beauty. The area has long been a subject of international geological debate, but it is thought that its complex formation is due to a period of volcanic activity followed by a period of glacial activity during successive ice ages. Its fathomless valleys, precipitous ridges, and craggy hills have taken eons to form.

The Ring of Gullion lies on the border between the south and north of Ireland, and it was once the edge of the Pale, the border of Norman Ireland. People have inhabited the area since the end of the last ice age, and evidence of ancient human settlement is seen in the smattering of stone tombs, including court tombs and portal tombs.

Ulster • Natural Wonders

146

In fact, the South Cairn at the summit of Slieve Gullion is the highest surviving passage tomb in Ireland.

The area is also steeped in legend, with it featuring in the Irish epic myth the *Táin Bó Cúailgne* showing demigod Cú Chulainn single-handedly defend Ulster from Queen Medb's army. Irish poet W.B. Yeats, acknowledging this link to ancient myth and literature, said that Slieve Gullion 'is perhaps the most mystic of our Irish mountains'.

The Slieve Gullion scenic drive is a great way to see the area in a short time, and it overlooks the Mourne Mountains, Armagh Drumlins, and Cooley Peninsula. There is also a way-marked trail for hikers, taking around four and a half hours, which brings you to the lake and the cairns on top of the mountain.

Beautiful landscape from the top of Slieve Gullion Forest Park.

80 Gleno Waterfall

Co. Antrim

The Gleno waterfall in Co. Antrim is one of Ireland's lesser-known natural wonders. It is almost 10 metres high and lies deep in the glens of Antrim. The trail to it is steep and can be muddy, but you will hear the rumbling of the waterfall nearby before it appears amid dense forest. You can view the waterfall from steps that have been constructed alongside it, or you can take a dip in its pool in summer when the water is still icy, but bearable.

The area is rich in flora and fauna, with oaks and rowans growing in the woodland and pine martens and buzzards making their homes there.

Ulster • Natural Wonders

The cascading waters of Gleno waterfall.

81 Slieve League Cliffs

Co. Donegal

The Slieve League Cliffs are on the southwest of Donegal, taking up some of Ireland's most spectacular coastline. They are 600 metres tall, almost three times the height of the Cliffs of Moher and among the highest accessible cliffs in Europe, delivering amazing views of Donegal Bay and the Atlantic Ocean. The cliffs were also an ancient pilgrimage site, and you can find the remains of a chapel and beehive huts on the mountain.

Right: Napoleonic watchtower on the sea cliffs at Slieve League, Donegal.

Below: A panoramic aerial view of the spectacular sea cliffs.

82 Lough Neagh

Northern Ireland

Lough Neagh is the largest lake in Ireland, with five of the six counties in Northern Ireland having shores on the lake. The vast waters contain several small islands, and its idyllic scenery is perfect for exploring from the land or by boat alike. It is a popular birdwatching spot, with a variety of birds nesting on the shores in both winter and summer, some of which have made an abandoned World War II torpedo testing platform on the lake their home.

Ulster • Natural Wonders

Right: Seagull looking at the camera and WW2 torpedo platform in the background in Lough Neagh.

Below: Lough Neagh at night.

83 *Titanic* Museum

Belfast

Opened in 2012, the *Titanic* Belfast is a worthy monument to the feat of building what was at the time the world's largest ship, and it is a poignant memorial to the tragedy of it sinking on its maiden voyage in 1912. It is located on the site of the former Harland & Wolff shipyard, where the RMS *Titanic* was built. The building itself is an eye-catching piece of architecture, with the shape mimicking that of the prow of *Titanic* and the height identical to the ship's hull.

Titanic was one of three Olympic-class ocean liners constructed in Belfast, the others being the *Olympic* and the *Brittanic*. All were designed to be the most luxurious passenger ships at the time, and the funnels on *Titanic* were wide enough to drive a train through. *Titanic* had a gym, smoking room, squash courts, a swimming pool, Turkish bath, and dog kennels. As well as carrying extremely wealthy, first-class passengers, the ship transported hundreds of emigrants. In fact, *Titanic's* proper name was 'Emigrant Ship Titanic', and it would never have been constructed without the record numbers of emigrants crossing the Atlantic. The 'RMS' preceding the ship's name stood for 'Royal Mail Steamer', as it was also intended to carry mail on its voyage.

The museum covers the history of *Titanic* from its inception to its tragic end, and some artefacts include one of the original life jackets and a pocket watch stopped at precisely 1:37 a.m. when it was submerged in the freezing ocean, which was owned by passenger Malcolm Joakim Johnson. The museum manages to pay suitable tribute to the many lives that were lost and tell the stories of survivors, while also celebrating the history of industrial Belfast and the phenomenal craftsmanship it took to build such an ambitious class of ships.

Ulster • Unique Ireland

Above: Titanic Belfast.

Below: RMS Titanic under construction.

155

84 Dunluce Castle

Co. Antrim

The haunting ruins of Dunluce Castle cling to a clifftop on the Causeway Coastal Route in Co. Antrim. The current structure dates back to around the 16th century, although there has been a castle there since the 13th century. The castle is flush up to the edge of the cliff, with plummeting slopes on either side, which was likely an important factor in the defence of the castle and part of the draw of the location.

Dunluce was subject to a history of warring clans, particularly the McQuillans and the MacDonnells. The McQuillans had been lords of the Route, a medieval territory on the northeast coast of Ulster, until they lost two major battles in the 16th century and were displaced by the MacDonnells. With deaths, marriages, and fighting in the clan, the castle passed through the hands of many, until the Glens of Antrim were seized in 1584 by Sorley Boy MacDonnell, who swore allegiance to Queen Elizabeth I and decided to renovate the castle in the Scottish style.

Not long after, in the early 1600s, a Spanish Armada warship was wrecked in a storm nearby, and the cannons from the ship were installed in the castle's gatehouses. Archaeological excavations in 2011 found evidence of a lost town (including indoor toilets!), which was obliterated during the Irish Rebellion of 1641, an uprising demanding greater Irish self-governance and an end to anti-Catholic discrimination.

With such a tumultuous history, Dunluce also has a fair share of folklore imprinted on its time-worn stone. It is said that Maeve Roe, thought to be the only daughter of Lord McQuillan, refused to marry the man her father had chosen for her as she was in love with someone else. Her father, furious, locked her in one of the turrets, but she escaped with her love only for the boat to capsize. And so was born the legend of Maeve, the Banshee of Dunluce Castle, whose wailing can be heard in the castle on stormy nights.

Dunluce Castle on the Causeway
Coastal Route in Co. Antrim.

85 Peace Walls

Belfast

The peace walls, or peace lines, of Northern Ireland were constructed after the 1969 Northern Ireland riots, an outbreak of civil and political unrest, which began in Derry on 12 August with the Battle of the Bogside, when nationalist residents of the Bogside area clashed with the RUC. The nationalist protests spread elsewhere in Northern Ireland and the British Army was deployed to extinguish them, with many people killed and hundreds injured.

Nationalist (and mostly Catholic) and loyalist (and mostly Protestant) communities in Northern Ireland were largely segregated, and the 'peace walls' were built where the two intersected in order to reduce tensions. The most well-known of these walls is at the intersection of the Falls Road and the Shankill Road in West Belfast, though there are many other walls, including the wall between Short Strand and Cluan Place in East Belfast, and others in Portadown and Derry. They range in length from a few hundred metres to a few kilometres.

Ulster • Unique Ireland

Intended to be a temporary measure, some of the walls have been standing for longer than the Berlin Wall, and they have increased in both number and height since the Good Friday Agreement in 1998. A lot of the walls are a canvas for Northern Ireland's colourful murals, which depict its political and cultural history. In 2013, the Northern Ireland Executive pledged to remove all peace walls by 2023, though few have been taken down. They are now a tourist attraction, where visitors can take a tour to appreciate the murals and learn what it was like to live in the shadow of the walls.

Above: Cupar Street in the Falls area. The tall brick wall is topped with a sheet metal partition that forms the 'peace line' in this part of Belfast.

Below: A colourful mural on a peace wall with portraits of historical figures.

86 Carrick-a-Rede Rope Bridge

Co. Antrim

The Carrick-a-Rede rope bridge, swaying almost 30 metres above the choppy water and only one metre wide, bridges the chasm between the mainland and Carrick-a-Rede Island. The island is an area of special scientific interest and it is home to a single building – a former salmon fisherman's cottage dating from the 1830s.

The bridge has existed in some form for over 250 years, with older bridges being no more than wooden slats and one rope rail. It is a safer construction now, though still a breathtaking experience to cross. It was originally constructed by fishermen, with the narrow gap between the two crops of land a bountiful place to catch salmon. There are few salmon to catch there today due to a decline in population, with almost 300 fish caught each day in the 1960s dwindling to only 250 over the whole season in the early 2000s. However, the landmark attracts hundreds of thousands of visitors each year to walk the short but dizzying (and very, very windy) bridge to the island.

Ulster • Unique Ireland

Carrick-a-Rede Island in Co. Antrim.
What better way to see it than by crossing
the rope bridge over the chasm below?

87 OM Dark Sky Park & Observatory

Co. Tyrone

Deep in Davagh Forest, this observatory is the first of its kind in Northern Ireland, with practically no light pollution allowing for clear skies to observe the stars and planets above. On the moorland in Beaghmore near the observatory, there are seven large stone circles, 10 stone rows, and 12 cairns, which were discovered in the 1930s by peat-cutters. In a beautiful synergy of ancestry and astronomy, some archaeologists believe the stones were constructed to track the movement of the sun and moon, with three of the stone rows aligning with the sunrise at solstice, meaning this place was as important for stargazing thousands of years ago as it is today.

The stone circle at Beaghmore early in the morning.

Ulster • Unique Ireland

Above: Night walks at the observatory. *Below:* On part of a sculpture trail, you will find a giant Ceoldán the Stargazer. Ceoldán is trying to capture the brilliance of the night sky.

88 Navan Fort

Co. Armagh

Navan Fort is an important archaeological site in Ireland, as well as appearing regularly in Irish myths, particularly the Ulster Cycle where it is the royal capital of Ulaidh and the seat of the Knights of the Red Branch. The site consists of a circular earthwork enclosure that's 250 metres in diameter. Excavation discovered tools and pottery dating to the Neolithic period. It also revealed that around the first century BC, a large timber structure was built and filled with thousands of stones before being deliberately burnt. The act appears to be a ritual, but the purpose of the building and burning remains a secret of the past.

Below: Navan Fort.   *Right:* Atmospheric view of part of the fort.

Ulster • Unique Ireland

89 Ards Forest Park

Co. Donegal

The unspoiled Ards Forest Park sits on a peninsula in Co. Donegal. Its 480 hectares covers a variety of habitats and landscapes, so you can enjoy both forest trails and beach walks in the same vicinity. The park was part of a country estate owned by the Stewart family until the early 1930s, but the forest park is now owned by Coillte, a state-owned commercial forestry business. There are both coniferous and deciduous woodlands, with oak, rowan, and ash among the trees that blanket the area. You'll find plenty of blackberry and bramble in the oak forest, and animals such as badgers, foxes, stoats, and hedgehogs have settled in the park.

The woodland comes right down to the shores of Lough Lilly, where you can spot white and yellow water lilies.

Aerial view of part of the park.

The salt marshes in the park are a Special Area of Conservation, as they're home to a variety of plant and animal life and an important wintering ground for birds. There is a bird hide at the end of the salt marsh trail where you can spend time observing the birds feeding and going about their business, an enjoyable watch whether you're an ornithologist or just a passer-by.

There are plenty of trails in the park, bringing you through the different habitats. The difficulty varies, with easier trails such as the Sand Dune Trail and the Green Walk or the more strenuous Binngorm Trail and Red Trail. There are also remains of ringforts and megalithic tombs in the park, with Irish legend saying that the tombs were the beds of the lovers Diarmuid and Gráinne. Apparently they stopped there when they ran away together because Gráinne didn't want to marry her betrothed, the warrior Fionn mac Cumhaill, who was older than her father.

90 Errigal

Co. Donegal

Errigal near Gweedore in Co. Donegal is the highest, and steepest, peak of the mountains known locally as the Seven Sisters, the others being Muckish, Crocknalaragagh, Aghla Beg, Ardloughnabrackbaddy, Aghla More, and Mackoght. The name 'Errigal' comes from the Old Irish 'airecal', meaning 'oratory', though there is a legend that the mountain was named by the Fir Bolg, the fourth group of people said to have settled in Ireland, who came from Greece to worship Errigal as they had Mount Olympus.

Errigal is 751 metres high and hiking it can take up to three hours, with its trail being a moderately challenging one. Part of the trail is marshy, with a section of scree towards the top that can be tricky on the way up as well as on the way down. At the top, there are amazing views of not just the Derryveagh Mountains in Donegal and the islands dotted along the coastline, but also Benbulben in Sligo. Errigal has twin summits, and there is a narrow pathway known as One Man's Pass that leads to the second, lower peak. The path is wide enough for one person to pass at a time, but it is worth taking a moment to stop at each peak and enjoy the scenery.

The foot of the mountain is surrounded by boglands, brimming with heather and gorse, and the snow-capped peak looks gorgeous in the winter. The best view of the mountain from afar, however, is during sunset, when its quartzite composition catches the light and the surface glows with a pinkish hue.

Ulster • The Great Outdoors

The beautiful Errigal reflected in the deep blue water below.

91 Mourne Mountains

Co. Down

The Mournes are the highest mountain range in Northern Ireland, with Slieve Donard its highest peak at 850 metres. On a clear day, the mountains can be seen from as far away as the Isle of Man. There are 12 mountains in the compact range, and they are designated an Area of Outstanding Natural Beauty.

The far-reaching Mournes have a wealth of hikes, with the lengthy Slieve Bearnagh trail probably the most unusual one. One of the mountain range's most unusual features, however, is the Mourne Wall, which took 18 years to complete. It is 35 kilometres long and crosses 15 peaks, including 7 of the 10 highest in the range. Some seasoned hikers have completed the Mourne Wall Walk, where they walk the entire route of the wall. It was built in the early 1900s when a reservoir was planned in the mountains, with the intention that the wall would keep farm animals away from the water. It was constructed from granite using traditional techniques, without the use of mortar.

The Silent Valley Reservoir remains today and is the main water supply for Co. Down. There is even a tunnel some 800 metres under Slieve Binnian, which was built to carry water to the reservoir.

While the peaks of the Mournes are a hiker's paradise, the foot of the mountains are surrounded by forests that offer more leisurely rambles. The beautiful Tollymore Forest Park has two rivers cutting through its towering trees, and its mossy rocks and old bridges give the forest an ethereal appearance. In fact, the Mourne Mountains served as an inspiration for C.S. Lewis' *The Chronicles of Narnia.*

Sunrise over the Mourne Mountains and lakes.

Ulster • The Great Outdoors

92 Murder Hole Beach (Boyeeghter Bay)

Co. Donegal

Officially called Boyeeghter Bay, the local name of 'Murder Hole Beach' is in stark opposition to its golden sands and idyllic surroundings. However, the waters are unpredictable, which may be part of the reason the beach has such an ominous name. At high tide, it is separated into two beaches, but it can be walked as one, long strand at low tide. There is a sea cave at the south section of the beach, which can also be accessed at low tide, but it's not advised. The tides rule on Murder Hole Beach, and its beauty is matched only by its treacherous riptides.

Murder Hole Beach, situated on the remote Rossguill Peninsula in Co. Donegal, is one of the most beautiful beaches in Ireland.

The sea cave at Murder Hole Beach.

93 The Gobbins

Co. Antrim

The Gobbins is a cliff path originally constructed by railway engineer Berkeley Deane Wise. It first opened in 1902, but fell into disrepair. Renovations were carried out in 2011, and a replica of the original Edwardian tubular bridge has been built for modern walkers. It is completely exposed to the elements, and, along with the other walkways and steps along the cliff face, it will bring you as close to where the sea meets land as you're likely to get.

Ulster • The Great Outdoors

Below: Part of the walkway clinging to the cliff.   *Opposite:* Metal gate at The Gobbins walk.

94 Cuilcagh Lakelands

Co. Fermanagh and Co. Cavan

Cuilcagh Lakelands is the world's first cross-border geopark, with the magnificent natural landscape spreading from Fermanagh in Northern Ireland to Cavan in the Republic. There is a bounty of things to explore, with rivers and drumlins to caves and cliffs. It is also a place of archaeological interest, and the area has an almost continuous history of settlement, with a Bronze Age wedge tomb called the Giant's Grave to be seen in the Cavan Burren Park.

Ulster • The Great Outdoors

People hiking on steep stairs of wooden boardwalk in Cuilcagh Mountain Park with a view of the lake and valley below.

95 Old Bushmills Distillery

Co. Antrim

Bushmills is the oldest licenced whiskey distillery in the world, and its operations remain in the village in Co. Antrim where it all began. In 1608, Sir Thomas Philips, an English knight who had been granted lands in Ulster, was given a licence to distil whiskey by King James I. The year 1608 appears on the labels of Bushmills whiskey, though the company wasn't formed until 1784 by a man called Hugh Anderson. Either way, the craft of distilling whiskey has been perfected over centuries, and the location of the distillery is imperative to the process, with water drawn from Saint Columb's Rill, a tributary of the River Bush, a key ingredient.

A devastating fire in 1885 saw the building burnt to the ground, but

Bushmills distillery building.

Ulster • Culture & Craic

it was rebuilt quickly and the company has been in near constant operation since. At the time, there was huge demand in the US for Irish whiskey, and Bushmills had their own steamship to transport the goods. The SS *Bushmills* made its maiden voyage in 1890, stopping at Philadelphia and New York City before sailing onwards to Singapore, Hong Kong, Shanghai, and Yokohama. The company's success in the US was almost scuppered by prohibition in the 1920s, but Bushmills' director at the time knew it would eventually come to an end, so they stockpiled whiskey. Their steamship set sail for Chicago on the repeal of prohibition with what was thought to have been the biggest shipment of whiskey ever to leave an Irish port.

The Old Bushmills Distillery provides an insight into history as well as their distillation process, with the company having been in existence throughout some of Ireland's most turbulent times. Its importance to the area was reflected in 2008 when an illustration of the distillery appeared on a series of sterling banknotes in Northern Ireland.

The bridge and river in Bushmills village in autumn.

96 Ulster Museum
Belfast

The Ulster Museum is the largest of the four national museums in Northern Ireland. It contains a vast number of objects over 8,000 square metres, spanning an impressive timescale from a 70-million-year-old dinosaur skeleton to contemporary fashion and textiles, including an exhibition of a *Game of Thrones* tapestry.

The museum was originally founded in 1821 as the Belfast Natural History Society, and its natural sciences collection has been built up for over a century. It includes the oldest rock in Ireland, which is from the island of Inishtrahull and almost 1.8 million years old. Its geological collection and the fossils they contain show how the climate has changed over thousands of years, and standing in its natural sciences section are two preserved skeletons of giant deer, often referred to as Irish elk.

The museum opened an art gallery in 1890, and its exhibitions now include works by Francis Bacon and the Northern Irish painter Marjorie Bloch. It has a large collection of fashion and textiles, with the museum collecting pieces ranging from early 20th-century Parisian couture to tapestries by Louis le Brocquy, and important pieces by Irish female embroiderers. The original textiles collection was destroyed in 1976 when Malone House in Belfast was bombed during the Troubles. The history of the Troubles, too, is covered in the museum, with its collection detailing the conflict and its impact on everyday life.

The range and eclecticism of the Ulster Museum means you can step into any point in history, with exhibits including Neolithic axe heads, an Egyptian mummy, Celtic art, treasure from the Spanish Armada, as well as an archive of books and manuscripts relating to Irish natural history on display.

Ulster Museum.

Ulster • Culture and Craic

97 Walled City of Derry

Derry–Londonderry

Derry is the only remaining completely walled city in Ireland, and the superbly intact circuit of ramparts stretch to about 1.5 kilometres in circumference. The walls can be walked, giving an ideal view of the historic city of Derry, which contains much of the county's most recognisable landmarks.

The walls were originally constructed between 1613 and 1619 by The Honourable The Irish Society, a London-based consortium of livery companies that was established during the Plantation of Ulster to assist with the colonisation of Derry. The previous settlement had been razed to the ground when Cahir O'Doherty, an Irish chieftain, led an army of rebels to attack the city. The walls were intended to protect the English and Scottish planters from other such attacks, and the city was officially renamed Londonderry in the royal charter – thus starting the long-lasting dispute over the county's name.

The strong walls of Derry have never been breached, even during the famous Siege of Derry in 1689. The siege was a result of the Williamite War in Ireland, with supporters of James II clashing with supporters of his successor, William of Orange. Thirteen apprentices locked the gates of the city to keep out forces who were loyal to James II. The siege continued for months, until a ship carrying supplies broke through the boom across the River Foyle and ended it.

The city's seven gates, four of which were built at the same time as the wall, are now very much open, with traffic signs to show height restrictions a modern addition. Its collection of 24 canons, which were well used during the siege, have also been restored to their former glory.

Ulster • Culture & Craic

Above: The City Walls of Derry are fortifications on the west bank of the River Foyle around the historic heart of the city.

Right: The armed merchant ship *Mountjoy* breaks through the defensive boom to relieve the Siege of Derry.

98 Ulster American Folk Park

Co. Tyrone

This open-air museum documents the lives of those who emigrated from Ulster to America between the 18th and 20th centuries. The Old World section of the park reenacts life at the time in Ulster, including streets of original houses, as well as demonstrations of blacksmithing and willow-weaving. The New World section recreates elements of an American street, with an Appalachian log house and a stone house, with the latter having been dismantled in America and painstakingly rebuilt in the folk park. The sections are joined by a full-size replica of an immigrant ship, the *Brig Union*, which visitors can board.

Two men play instruments at Ulster American Folk Park in Northern Ireland.

Ulster • Culture and Craic

Above: Appalachian-styled timber houses.

Below: The *Brig Union.*

99 Alcorn's Tropical World

Co. Donegal

In Alcorn's Flower & Garden Centre, hundreds of butterflies create a kaleidoscopic display as they flit about the renowned butterfly house. There is also a mini zoo, with colourful and exotic birds such as lorikeets and turacos as well as meerkats and lemurs. It is an unlikely trip to the tropics in the heart of Letterkenny, closed during winter.

Two beautiful Glasswing butterflies from Central and Southern America, so called because of their transparent wings.

Ulster • Culture and Craic

100 North West 200

The Triangle, Northern Ireland

The North West 200 is an
annual motorcycle race, with a
circuit that connects the towns
of Portstewart, Coleraine and
Portrush. First held in 1929, it
now attracts over 150,000 visitors
wanting to witness one of the
fastest courses in the world.
The circuit is mostly made up of
public roads, and race week has
an array of events that include
concerts and stunt shows.

Right: Competitors in action.

Below: The course by the rugged coastline
of Co. Antrim and the Atlantic Ocean.

101 Belfast International Arts Festival

Belfast

This annual festival was first started in 1962 by a student, and it was originally hosted by Queen's University. It is now a three-week long event usually held in October and November in over 30 venues across Belfast, showcasing the best of homegrown and international talent working in the arts.

Glen Hansard at Belfast International Arts Festival.

Ulster • Culture & Craic

Above and below: Cristal Palace by Transe Express at Belfast
International Arts Festival 2022 in Belfast Titanic Quarter.

Index

Picture credits

The publisher gratefully acknowledges the following image copyright holders. All images are copyright © individual rights holders unless stated otherwise. Every effort has been made to trace copyright holders, or copyright holders not mentioned here. If there have been any errors or omissions, the publisher would be happy to rectify this in any reprint.

1 Lauren Radley	73 Michael Diggin	136 Brigit's Garden (all)
3 Sean O' Dwyer / Shutterstock	74 MNStudio / Shutterstock	137 Mark Gusev / Shutterstock
7 Shutterupeire / Shutterstock	77 Dawid K Photography / Shutterstock	138 The Galway International Oyster & Seafood
8 Agaglowala / Shutterstock	79 Mark Gusev / Shutterstock	Festival /Declan Colohan
11 Shawnwil23 / Shutterstock	80 Piotr Machowczyk / Shutterstock	139 The Galway International Oyster & Seafood
13 Michael Diggin	81 H4 PH / Shutterstock	Festival / Declan Colohan (all)
15 Frank33 / Dreamstime	82 Oliver Heinrichs / Shutterstock	140 Stephen Lavery / Depositphotos
17 Derick P. Hudson / Shutterstock	83 David Ribeiro / Dreamstime (all)	140 Meunierd / Dreamstime
18 Kris Dublin / Shutterstock	85 National Library of Wales	141 Claude Arcadie / Shutterstock
18 Viorel Dudau / Dreamstime	85 Kwiatek7 / Shutterstock	141 Francesco Ricciardi Exp / Shutterstock
19 Abitofeverything / Shutterstock	87 Faysal06 / Shutterstock	143 Puripat Lertpunyaroj / Dreamstime
19 Licht und Schatten / Shutterstock	89 Roland Paschhoff (all)	145 Irina Wilhauk / Shutterstock
21 Jan-Philipp Litza / Creative Commons	90 Pensell Photography / Shutterstock	146 Pavel Voitukovic / Shutterstock
22 Peter Krocka / Shutterstock	92 David Lippincott	147 Harry Welsh007 / Dreamstime
23 Hordinsky Photography / Shutterstock	93 Pierre Leclerc / Shutterstock	150 Mark Carthy / Dreamstime
24 Gigashots / Shutterstock	94 Darragh Kane	151 Stephen Barnes / Shutterstock
27 Irina Wilhauk / Shutterstock	96 Shawn Williams / Dreamstime	152 Michael McGlinchey / Shutterstock
29 Niall Carson / PA / Alamy	96 Debra Reschoff Ahearn / Dreamstime	153 Mert Cetinkaya / Alamy Stock Photo
30 Lukas Bischoff / Shutterstock	97 Attila Jandi / Dreamstime	155 Nataliya Hora / Shutterstock
33 O Kelly / Stockimo / Alamy	97 The Galway International Oyster & Seafood	155 Meunierd / Dreamstime
34 Walshphotos / Shutterstock	Festival / Declan Colohan	156 Jan Miko / Shutterstock
35 Kim Haughton / Alamy Stock Photo	99 Legend Images / Alamy Stock Photo	158 Meunierd / Dreamstime
36 Kirk Fisher / Shutterstock	100 Alexilena	159 Avillphoto / Shutterstock
37 Derick P. Hudson / Shutterstock	102 Pekinnaird / Shutterstock	161 Lautz / Shutterstock
38 Michael Cash Photography / Shutterstock	103 Judith Lienert / Shutterstock	162 JRP Studio / Shutterstock
41 Pablescu / Shutterstock	104 Davide Savio	163 OM Dark Sky Park & Observatory
43 RM Floral / Alamy Stock Photo	106 David Soanes / Shutterstock	163 OM Dark Sky Park & Observatory
44 Peter Krocka / Shutterstock	108 Dawid K Photography / Shutterstock	164 Claude Arcadie / Shutterstock
45 Michael Diggin	109 Patrick Mangan / Shutterstock	164 Dreamstime.com
47 Colin / Wikimedia Commons	111 Tony Potter	166 Thomas Lukassek / Dreamstime
49 Wirestock Creators / Shutterstock	112 Maksana Photo / Shutterstock	169 Michael Diggin
51 Dawid K Photography / Shutterstock	115 Michael Murtagh / Creative Commons	171 Sara Winter / Dreamstime
52 Sean's Bar	116 Bob Hilscher / Shutterstock	172 Gazzag / Dreamstime
53 Danita Delimont / Alamy	117 Stefanovalerigm / Dreamstime	173 Babett Paul / Dreamstime
54 Al Teich / Shutterstock	118 Teapot Press	174 Ingrid Pakats / Shutterstock
55 National Gallery of Ireland	118 Mark Gusev / Shutterstock	175 Eakachai Leesin / Dreamstime
56 Michael Diggin	120 Mica Stock / Shutterstock	177 Dawid Kalisinski / Dreamstime
56 Foynes Flying Boat & Maritime Museum	121 Mica Stock / Shutterstock	178 Wilfred de Vampo / Dreamstime
57 Michael Diggin	122 Matthi / Shutterstock	179 Ledokol / Dreamstime
57 Darragh Kane Photography	123 Mica Stock / Shutterstock	181 Claudiodivizia / Dreamstime
58 Kwiatek7	124 Three Sixty Images / Shutterstock	183 Shawnwil23 / Shutterstock
61 Michael Diggin	127 Eamonn McCarthy / Shutterstock	183 British Library / Creative Commons
63 Corey Macri / Shutterstock	127 Stephen Barnes / Shutterstock	184 Jingmin310 / Dreamstime
64 dvlcom / www.dvlcom.co.uk	127 Frank Bach / Shutterstock	185 Peter Steele / Dreamstime
65 DejaVuDesign / Shutterstock	128 PJ Photography / Shutterstock	185 Peter Steele / Dreamstime
67 Rui Vale Sousa / Shutterstock	129 Lisandro Luis Trarbach / Shutterstock	186 Albert Beukhof / Shutterstock
69 Seanfitz09 / Shutterstock	130 Jean-Michel Desert / Shutterstock	187 Paul
71 Foynes Flying Boat & Maritime Museum	131 Andrea Rusconi / Shutterstock	187 Ballygally View Images
71 Foynes Flying Boat & Maritime Museum	132 Unknown	188 Belfast International Arts Festival /
72 Umomos / Shutterstock	133 Natalia Paklina / Shutterstock	Simon Hutchinson
73 Irish Drone Photography / Shutterstock	135 Jakub Wojciechowski / Shutterstock	189 Belfast International Arts Festival /
		Johnny Frazer (all)

SOLOHEAD
IRISH CREAMERY BUTTER
CO-OPERATIVE AGRICULTURAL & DAIRY SOCIETY, LTD.
LIMERICK
JUNCTION

CREAMERY IRISH BUTTER
CAPPAMORE
CO-OP AGRICULTURAL & DAIRY SOC. LTD.
CAPPAMORE, Co. LIMERICK.

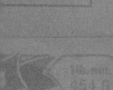

BLACK SWAN

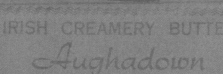

IRISH CREAMERY BUTTER
Aughadown
MANUFACTURED BY
WEST CORK CREAMERIES,
AUGHADOWN, SKIBBEREEN

REG Nº C.115

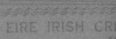

EIRE IRISH CRE
Dick
CREAMERY
FARRANFOR

É
Irish Cream
KENMARE
KENMARE,
Reg. No. C219